A STUDY GUIDE COMMENTARY

EXODUS

BOOKS IN THE "STUDY GUIDE" SERIES . . .

A STUDY GUIDE
COMMENTARY

EXODUS

F. B. HUEY JR.

ZONDERVAN
PUBLISHING HOUSE

OF THE ZONDERVAN CORPORATION
GRAND RAPIDS, MICHIGAN 49506

Exodus: A Study Guide Commentary
© 1977 by The Zondervan Corporation
Grand Rapids, Michigan

Library of Congress Cataloging in Publication Data

Huey, F   B   1925-
  Exodus: a study guide commentary.

  Bibliography: p.
  1. Bible. O.T. Exodus—Commentaries.   I. Bible.
O.T. Exodus. 1977. English.   II. Title.
BS1245.3.H83   222'.12'07   77-9995

ISBN 0-310-36053-6

Printed in the United States of America

Contents

Introduction

A. Importance of the Book of Exodus

Any list of the three or four most important books of the Old Testament would include the Book of Exodus, the second book in the Old Testament. The Exodus experience is to the Old Testament and Judaism what the Cross in the New Testament is to the Christian faith. The Exodus is the climactic event of Hebrew history, when God acted to deliver His people from bondage, just as the Cross is the central event of Christian history, when God acted to deliver mankind from the bondage of sin.

This book develops some of the most important theological themes in the Old Testament: redemption, salvation, election, worship, law, covenant, and priesthood. The Exodus has been called a paradigm of the Christian faith (i.e., a parallel of Christian experience): bondage, deliverance, wandering, and the Promised Land.

B. Name of the Book

It was a common practice in the ancient Near East to name a book by its first word or first significant phrase. The Book of Exodus is called *we'elleh sh^emoth* in the Hebrew Bible. These are the first two words of the book, and they mean "and these are the names." When the Hebrew Bible was translated into the Greek language, new names were given to the first five books of the Old Testament. The second book was called "Exodus" from two Greek words, *ek* (meaning "out of" or "from") and *'odos* (meaning "a road" or "traveled way"). Therefore, the title means "a road out" or "departure," and describes the central event of the book — the departure of the Hebrew people from Egypt. The word that became the title given by the Greek translators is found in Exodus 19:1 ("when

7

the children of Israel *were gone forth"*). The Latin Vulgate called it *Liber Exodi,* from which the title comes into the English language as the Book of Exodus.

Though the English title, Exodus, is more appropriate than the Hebrew title, "and these are the names," it does not cover the subject matter of the entire book but only of the first fifteen chapters. The larger part of the book deals with the establishing and ordering of daily life of the Hebrew people through various laws given at Mount Sinai and contains extensive instructions for the building of the tabernacle and the ministry of the priests.

C. Authorship

For almost 1800 years of the Christian era, there was little doubt expressed about the Mosaic authorship of the Pentateuch (another name for the first five books of the Old Testament). However, influenced by Julius Wellhausen and other critical scholars of the nineteenth century, all but the most conservative scholars abandoned belief in Mosaic authorship during the first half of the twentieth century. Principal arguments used by conservative scholars who have continued to support Mosaic authorship are: (1) Jesus Himself affirmed that Moses was the author (Mark 10:4,5; Luke 24:44; John 5:46,47, etc.); (2) Moses was qualified by background and training to be its author; (3) certain parts claim to have been written by Moses (Exod. 17:14; 24:4; 34:27,28; Num. 33:2; Deut. 31:9,22,24-26); (4) ancient Jewish tradition holds that he was the author; and (5) archaeological discoveries have confirmed the accuracy of customs, events, and names that are found in the Pentateuch and suggest that the author was not writing hundreds of years after the event.

Presently there seems to be a growing conviction that the tradition of Mosaic authorship of the Pentateuch is not an invention, and even the most liberal scholars have conceded that at least some parts of the Pentateuch can be traced back to Moses.[1] Perhaps an observation by John Calvin could best settle the ongoing debate on authorship of certain books of the Bible: "Men have not invented what is contained in the Old and New Testaments . . . God is the real author." If we affirm that Exodus, or any other book of the Bible, was written under the

---

[1]For a defense of the traditional Mosaic authorship of the Pentateuch, read T. W. Wenham, "Moses and the Pentateuch," in *The New Bible Commentary: Revised*, eds. D. Guthrie and J. A. Motyer (Grand Rapids: Wm. B. Eerdmans Publishing Company, 1970), pp. 41-43.

inspiration of the Spirit of God, then disputes among scholars as to the exact name of the author become largely academic and of secondary importance.

D. Date of the Exodus

Even if all scholars agreed that Moses wrote the Book of Exodus, there still would remain the unresolved question of when the events took place. Old Testament writers did not record history as we do. They were not always concerned about giving names of foreign rulers or exact dates of events, and so the chronology of the Old Testament, particularly before the establishment of the monarchy, is not always easy to reconstruct. If only the name of the pharaoh of the first chapter of Exodus had been mentioned by name just once, how many questions raised by historians would have been laid to rest!

There is no extrabiblical or archaeological evidence and nothing in the Egyptian records that make mention of the Exodus. There are no extant historical documents that enable us to pinpoint the date of the Exodus. Scholars are divided into two principal camps on this question: some support an earlier date (around 1440 B.C., during the eighteenth Egyptian dynasty), and others support a later date (around 1280 or 1230 B.C., during the nineteenth dynasty).[2] It seems that for every argument supporting either date there is a counterargument of equal merit. Therefore, final determination of the actual date of the Exodus must wait for further evidence that will shed more light on the problem.

E. Historicity of the Exodus

Regardless of our inability to pinpoint the date of the Exodus, it was a historical event. Though none of the extensive Egyptian records mentions a revolt of a group of slaves and their escape from the country, this lacuna should not be surprising. The event was a defeat for the Egyptian army and the Egyptian people. Rulers of nations prefer to commemorate victories, not reverses or humiliating defeats. Nor was the escape of the Israelite slaves considered theologically significant by

---

[2]For detailed studies of the date of the Exodus the reader is referred to: R. K. Harrison, *Introduction to the Old Testament* (Grand Rapids: William B. Eerdmans Publishing Company, 1969), pp. 315-325; Gabriel Hebert, *When Israel Came Out of Egypt* (Richmond: John Knox Press, 1961), pp. 44-50; J. W. Jack, *The Date of the Exodus* (Edinburgh: T. and T. Clark, 1925); K. A. Kitchen, *Ancient Orient and Old Testament* (Chicago: InterVarsity Press, 1966). pp. 57-75; H. H. Rowley, *From Joseph to Joshua* (London: Oxford University Press, 1950).

the Egyptians, any more than the crucifixion of Jesus by the Roman soldiers. To the Romans it was just another execution of a troublesome Jew, not worth recording in any Roman documents that have survived. The real import of the Exodus surely escaped the Egyptians, also.

No tradition as lasting as this would be without historical basis, nor would the Israelite people have invented such a shameful and ignominious episode as part of its national history. A fictionalized account of one's ancestors would depict their origins as much more noble and heroic. The faith of Israel finds its origin in a historical Exodus experience and is dependent upon its reality.

F. Outline of the Book

The Book of Exodus may be divided into four major parts: Part One: Israel in Egypt (chaps. 1-11); Part Two: Deliverance From Egypt (chaps. 12-18); Part Three: A New Relationship (chaps. 19-31); Part Four: Rebellion and Renewal (chaps. 32-40). These four major divisions are further subdivided, and the chapter divisions of this study follow these subdivisions.

Part One: Israel in Egypt (1:1–11:10)

Chapter 1: Oppression of the Hebrews in Egypt (1:1–2:25)
A. Beginning of the oppression (1:1-22)
1. Rapid increase of the Hebrews (1:1-7)
2. Enslavement of the people (1:8-14)
3. Slaying of the male children (1:15-22)
B. Provision by God of a leader (2:1-25)
1. Birth and adoption of Moses (2:1-10)
2. Murder of an Egyptian (2:11-14)
3. Flight to Midian (2:15-25)

Chapter 2: The Call of Moses (3:1–4:17)
A. Words from a burning bush (3:1-10)
1. Self-revelation of God (3:1-6)
2. God's plan for deliverance (3:7-10)
B. Excuses of a reluctant servant (3:11–4:12)
1. Not capable to do the task (3:11,12)
2. No knowledge of God's name (3:13-22)
3. People who will not believe (4:1-9)
4. Inability to speak eloquently (4:10-12)
C. Moses' refusal and God's anger (4:13-17)

Chapter 3: Preparations for Deliverance (4:18–7:7)
  A. Moses' return to Egypt (4:18-31)
    1. Departure from Midian (4:18-23)
    2. Circumcision of Moses' son (4:24-26)
    3. Israel's acceptance of Moses' leadership (4:27-31)
  B. First confrontation with Pharaoh (5:1–6:13)
    1. Pharaoh's scorn (5:1-9)
    2. The people's workload increased (5:10-14)
    3. Complaints directed to Moses by the people (5:15-21)
    4. Complaints directed to God by Moses (5:22,23)
    5. God's assurance of victory (6:1-13)
  C. Parenthetical (6:14–7:7)
    1. The genealogy of Moses and Aaron (6:14-27)
    2. The call of Moses retold (6:28–7:7)

Chapter 4: The Confrontation With Pharaoh (7:8–11:10)
  A. Signs of power given to Moses (7:8-13)
  B. The plagues (7:14–11:10)
    1. Water changes to blood (7:14-25)
    2. Frogs fill the land (8:1-15)
    3. Gnats cover man and beast (8:16-19)
    4. Flies swarm throughout the land (8:20-32)
    5. Disease inflicts the animals (9:1-7)
    6. Boils break out on man and beast (9:8-12)
    7. Hail shatters the land (9:13-35)
    8. Locusts cover the land (10:1-20)
    9. Darkness envelops the land (10:21-29)
    10. Death announced for the firstborn (11:1-10)

Part Two: Deliverance From Egypt (12:1–18:27)
Chapter 5: The Passover and Departure from Egypt (12:1–15:21)
  A. Institution of the Passover (12:1-36)
    1. Instructions for the first Passover (12:1-13)
    2. Instructions for Feast of Unleavened Bread (12:14-20)
    3. Observance of the first Passover (12:21-36)
  B. Israel's departure from Egypt (12:37-51)
  C. Dedication of the firstborn (13:1-16)
  D. Crossing of the Red Sea (13:17–15:21)
    1. Divine guidance by day and night (13:17-22)
    2. Pursuit by Pharaoh (14:1-14)

PART ONE: ISRAEL IN EGYPT

Chapter 1

Oppression of the Hebrews in Egypt

(Exodus 1:1–2:25)

The best introduction to the Book of Exodus is the Book of Genesis, particularly chapters 37–50. The story of Joseph found in these chapters sets the stage for what follows in Exodus, and the reader would be at a loss to know why the Israelites were in Egypt without them. The first chapter of Exodus is not the beginning of a new story but the continuation of the last chapter of Genesis.

A. Beginning of the Oppression (1:1-22)

1. *Rapid increase of the Hebrews* (1:1-7)

The first six verses of Exodus summarize in a few words the story of Joseph and explain how the Israelites came to be in Egypt. In the full account in Genesis 37-50 we are told that in God's providence Joseph, who had been sold into slavery by his jealous brothers, rose to prominence in Egypt so that when his brothers came there seeking food in a time of famine, the one whose life they had loathed was now in a position to save their lives by giving them the food they needed. A forgiving Joseph invited his father, brothers, and their families, totaling seventy members, to dwell in Goshen (usually identified as the Wadi Tumilat, the eastern part of the Nile delta) for the remainder of the famine years. The number seventy did not include the wives of Jacob's sons, but did include Joseph and his two sons, who were already in Egypt (Gen. 46:26,27; cf. Deut. 10:22).

Like relatives who come to visit for a few days but prolong the visit indefinitely, Jacob's family did not return to Canaan after the famine but remained in Egypt for 430 years (Exod. 12:40). Their number grew so great that the Egyptians began to fear them. In describing their growth, verse 7 intentionally repeats three words used in Genesis 1:20-22:

"fruitful . . . increased abundantly . . . multiplied." The word "increased abundantly" is used in the Old Testament to describe teeming hordes of marine or animal life (Gen. 1:20; 7:21). The Israelites had become as thick as flies in the land! The stage was now set for the first Jewish persecution in history.

2. Enslavement of the people (1:8-14)

Joseph and his family had been welcome guests in Egypt, but many years passed, and a pharaoh (a title of respect that means "great house") came to the throne "who knew not Joseph," i.e., did not remember with gratitude what Joseph had done for Egypt. His identity is dependent upon establishment of the date of the Exodus (see Introduction for discussion of date). This pharaoh was fearful that the Israelites might ally themselves with the enemy if there was an invasion. Also, they had become an economic asset, and he was afraid they might decide to leave the country. So he enslaved them and placed heavy burdens on them that included the building of the store cities of Pithom and Raamses (sites for the storage of government supplies, agricultural products, military equipment, etc.). Pithom usually is identified with Tell el-Maskhuta in the Wadi Tumilat, or Tell er-Retabeh, about nine miles to the west. Raamses (or Rameses) usually is identified with modern San el-Hajar, believed to be the ancient site of Avaris (also called Tanis). Others identify with Qantir, fifteen miles to the south. The Israelites also were forced to make bricks, construct dams and irrigation canals, and carry out other building projects of the ambitious pharaoh. By making them serve "with rigour" (1:14; the Hebrew word means "to break" or "crush in pieces"), he hoped to reduce their numbers. Instead, they continued to increase.

3. Slaying of the male children (1:15-22)

When the pharaoh saw that oppressive work heaped on the Israelites did not stop their increase, he determined to take even more drastic measures to destroy them. First, he sought the cooperation of the Hebrew midwives to kill the male babies while the mothers were still on the birthstool (1:16; probably stones on which the Hebrew women sat or knelt while giving birth, a common practice in the ancient Near East). The midwives "feared God" (1:17; "fear" in the Hebrew language can express the idea of worship, obedience, or faith, as well as dread) and would not kill the newborn male children. How strange that the names of the two humble midwives, Shiphrah and Puah, Semitic names that mean "beauty" and "splendor," are preserved in the Scriptures, but not the name of the mighty pharaoh. They told the pharaoh that the Hebrew women were so vigorous that the babies were already born before they could arrive to carry out his orders. God rewarded the midwives for their compassion by giving them families of their own (1:21). The infuriated pharaoh then ordered his people to cast every male Hebrew baby into the Nile, an effort that eventually would have resulted in the total extermination of the Israelites if carried out. In his rage he seemed to forget their economic worth to his nation and was now determined to get rid of all of them.

B. Provision by God of a Leader (2:1-25)

1. *Birth and adoption of Moses* (2:1-10)

The focus of the agony of the Hebrew people now shifts to one family. A man from the Levite tribe married a kinswoman. In Exodus 6:20 and Numbers 26:59 the couple are identified as Amram and Jochebed, the latter the sister of Amram's father, a relationship that would make Moses' mother also his great-aunt! Though the narrative begins with the account of Moses' birth, Amram and Jochebed already had two other children, Miriam and Aaron, both of whom had been born before the murderous decree was issued. Because of the failure to mention the other children at this point in the narrative (though the text does not say that Moses was the firstborn), some have concluded that Miriam and Aaron were Amram's children by a previous marriage. In support of the theory it has been noted that Miriam is sometimes called "Aaron's sister" (15:20), but never "Moses' sister." However, Numbers 26:59 clearly identifies her as sister of both Aaron and Moses. Exodus 7:7 tells us that Aaron was three years older than Moses, and Miriam is identified by name for the first time in 15:20.

When Moses was too large to be hidden any longer, the mother made a basket (2:3; a word that is used elsewhere in the Old Testament only of Noah's ark) of bulrushes (or papyrus, which commonly grew along the banks of the Nile and was used by the Egyptians for making paper, baskets, and boats of various kinds). She daubed it with bitumen ("slime," KJV) and pitch to make it watertight and then placed it among the reeds at the river's bank. It would appear that she was abandoning the child to his fate (a practice called "exposure" in the ancient world, common even among the cultured Greeks when they wanted to get rid of unwanted babies). However, his sister Miriam remained hidden nearby to see what would happen to him, an act that suggests the family had not totally abandoned him but had hope that some compassionate person would find him.

God's plan for the deliverance of His people was now reduced to the slender thread of a tiny baby under a decree of death set adrift on a river in a fragile basket. Hundreds of years later His plan for the deliverance of mankind would again be reduced to the slender thread of a tiny baby, this time in a manger in Bethlehem (Luke 2:1-20).

The baby was discovered by Pharaoh's daughter when she came with her maidens to bathe in the river, a practice verified by Egyptian monuments that show ladies of high rank, with their female servants, bathing in the Nile. Many attempts have been made to identify this unnamed princess. The Pseudepigrapha calls her Tharmuth (Jub. 47:5); Josephus called her Thermuthis; the historian Eusebius called her Merris, and the Talmud, Bithiah. She has been identified as the remarkable feminist Queen Hatshepsut, half-sister of Thutmosis III, whose statues from her temple at Deir el-Bahri represent her as a male ruler with the full pharaonic regalia, including the customary artificial chinbeard! She also has been identified as one of Rameses II's fifty-nine daughters, but until the pharaoh himself can be identified with certainty, the daughter's identity is even more problematic.

The princess recognized Moses as one of the Hebrew babies, took pity on him, and determined to raise him as her own son, in apparent disobedience to her own father's decree to kill the Hebrew babies. Miriam emerged from her hiding place and offered to find a nurse from the Hebrew women for the baby. The princess agreed, and the happy child took the infant to his own mother. Thus Moses' life was saved, and he was reunited with his mother during his childhood years.

The meaning of the name given to the baby by Pharaoh's daughter has occasioned much discussion. It has been identified as a participial form of a Hebrew word *mashah* meaning "to draw out," which according to the text (2:10, "because I drew him out of the water") is the reason the princess called him Moses. However, because it seems strange that an Egyptian princess would give her adopted child a Hebrew name, most scholars have concluded that the name is from an Egyptian word *ms(w)* that means "to give birth" and appears in many Egyptian names (e.g., Thutmosis, "Thoth is born"; Rameses). The argument by some scholars that the princess could not have known any Hebrew words cannot stand up under careful scrutiny. Such ignorance would be as unlikely as a person living in the southwestern United States not knowing a single word of Spanish. If the princess was strong-willed enough to defy her father's decree by adopting a Hebrew baby, it is not impossible that she gave him a Hebrew name, knowing he was a Hebrew.

2. Murder of an Egyptian (2:11-14)

All the years of Moses' youth are passed over in silence. Answers to questions such as "When did Moses discover he was a Hebrew?" "Did his mother instruct him in the faith of her ancestors?" "When did he first have inner stirrings that he would be the deliverer of his people?" can only be guesses at best. Such omissions that would seem inexcusable to the logic of a twentieth-century writer of history are characteristic of the Bible. Details are omitted, events are telescoped or passed over altogether, for the attention of the biblical writers was always centered on God's plan of redemption as it was being revealed through the history of Israel. All other events and people were peripheral or unimportant for their purposes. All that is known about Moses' formative years is found in Acts 7:22: "Moses was educated in all the wisdom of the Egyptians and was powerful in speech and action" (NIV).

The story of Moses continues "when Moses was grown" (2:11). Acts 7:23 tells us that he was now forty years of age. Hebrews 11:24,25 adds that at this time "By faith Moses, when he had grown up, refused to be known as the son of Pharaoh's daughter. He chose to be mistreated along with the people of God rather than to enjoy the pleasures of sin for a short time" (NIV). The oppression of the Israelites had not abated in the intervening years. One day Moses witnessed an Egyptian beating a Hebrew and was so enraged that he killed the Egyptian on the spot and buried him, thinking that no one saw the deed. The next day he saw two Hebrews fighting each other and tried to stop the fight. They both turned on him and repudiated his attempt to mediate the dispute with the stinging words, "Who made thee a prince and a judge over us?" (2:14) and then sarcastically asked if he planned to kill them as he had killed the Egyptian. This would not be the last time his own people would challenge Moses' authority over them.

3. Flight to Midian (2:15-25)

News of the murder also soon reached the ears of Pharaoh, and in his wrath he determined to kill Moses. Murder by members of the royal family would not ordinarily have been punishable by death, because Pharaoh was a law unto himself (no written law codes have ever been found in Egypt, as in other ancient Near Eastern civilizations, as Pharaoh's word was the only law). It is unlikely that this one deed would have incited Pharaoh's anger against a member of his own household. Therefore, we can only conclude that Pharaoh had never really accepted Moses as a member of his family and was only waiting for the right opportunity to take revenge on this one who had escaped his decree of execution as a baby.

The question of the rightness or wrongness of the slaying of an Egyptian by Moses cannot be ignored. Though our sympathies may be with Moses and his oppressed people, can violence or killing, even for a "good cause," ever be justified? The pages of history are stained with the blood of those killed in the name of "good causes" and of religion, even the Christian religion. Moses would be the deliverer of his people, but he was going about it the wrong way; murder was no way to redeem Israel.

Moses fled to the land of Midian (2:15), a geographical region whose exact location is uncertain. It has been identified with northwestern Arabia, on the east shore of the Gulf of Aqaba to the south of Palestine. However, the Midianites were seminomadic and probably should not be identified with a specific territory. There is evidence that some of them moved about and settled in the Sinai peninsula area.

While sitting at a well resting from his journey across the desert from Egypt, Moses witnessed seven daughters of a priest of Midian come to the well to draw water for their father's flock (Arab women, never the men, still draw water for the flocks in Israel and Jordan). Shepherds came to drive them away to get the scarce water for their own flocks. Consistent with his concern for the oppressed, Moses intervened and even helped the daughters water their flock. When the daughters returned home, they told their father Reuel (also called Jethro, 3:1;[1] Hobab, Judg. 4:11; but cf. Num. 10:29 where Hobab is called the son of Raguel) what had happened. He rebuked his daughters for forgetting the customary hospitality that would have required them to invite the stranger home with them. Moses came to live with the family, and one of the daughters, Zipporah (a name that means "bird"), was given to him in

---

[1]Also called Jether (4:18) according to Hebrew spelling, but English translations change it to read "Jethro" to conform with all other occurrences of this name.

marriage. Their first son was named Gershom (from a word meaning "to drive out," or from two words that mean "sojourner there"); either interpretation would recall the experiences that brought Moses to live with the Midianite priest and his family). A second son, not mentioned until later (18:4), was named Eliezer.

The identity of the priest of Midian has for some time been of interest to scholars. In Judges 1:16 and 4:11 he is described as a member of a Kenite family (the same Hebrew word is used also for Cain, the first son of Adam and Eve). Therefore, it is correct to say he was a Kenite serving as a priest among the Midianites and was not one of them. In Genesis 25:2 Midian is listed as a child of Keturah, Abraham's second wife. Is it possible that belief in God had been passed down to these seminomadic people through the descendants of Midian, just as this same belief had been passed down through another branch of the family, Abraham's son Isaac by his first wife, and through him to Jacob and the Israelites who were now living in Egypt? If so, Reuel and his family, and probably the Midianites, were already worshipers of God when Moses arrived to live among them. In further support of this possibility, Moses' father-in-law, exercising his priestly function, offered sacrifices to God when Moses returned to Sinai with the liberated Israelites (18:12). Scholars refer to this link between Reuel and the God of the Israelites as "The Kenite Hypothesis" and suggest that Moses may have come to know about God first through his father-in-law (rather than through his mother in Egypt).

It has been previously noted that a gap of forty years' silence occurred between verses 10 and 11. Now another forty years of Moses' life is passed over in silence between verses 22 and 23 (cf. 7:7 and Acts 7:30). The pharaoh who had oppressed the Israelites so cruelly died after a long reign, paving the way for Moses to return to Egypt. God had not forgotten His people, nor had He forgotten Moses, who would still be their deliverer. Verses 24 and 25 with their emphasis on four verbs set the stage for the dramatic encounter between God and Moses in the next chapter: "God heard . . . God remembered . . . God saw . . . God knew . . ." (KJV translates the last word "had respect," but the Hebrew word is "knew," a word that can imply the most intimate kind of knowledge; cf. Gen. 4:1).

The seeming silence of God for forty years did not mean that He had forgotten His people or His covenant with Abraham. During the two most agonizing experiences of His earthly life — Gethsemane and the cross — our Lord also was greeted only by the silence of God, and yet God could never have been any closer to His son than on those two occasions. The silences of God do not mean that He is inactive or impotent; they may be the times He is working most actively on behalf of His people. Moses would soon learn this truth at a burning bush.

For Further Study

1. In a Bible dictionary or encyclopedia (see bibliography) read articles on Egypt, Moses, slavery.

2. Is violence ever justified for the Christian?

3. Why did God allow His people to remain in bondage such a long time (more than eighty years) before sending them a deliverer?

4. Though we sympathize with Moses' reaction when he saw an Egyptian beating a Hebrew, murder must always be considered a sin. How many other great figures of the Old Testament can you think of who committed sins in violation of God's laws? What lessons can be learned from their lapses?

5. If as a Christian you found yourself subject to persecution, what do you think your reaction would be?

Chapter 2

The Call of Moses

(Exodus 3:1–4:17)

Moses sinned when he killed an Egyptian, and as a consequence he suffered forty years of separation from his people and family. Whatever stirrings he had once felt in his heart for his oppressed people had surely been buried in the past, and he had long since settled down to a shepherd's life among the Midianites with the family of Jethro the priest. But God had not forgotten Moses. He was now ready to appear to Moses and call him to his new task.

A. Words From a Burning Bush (3:1-10)

1. *Self-revelation of God* (3:1-6)

One day while tending his father-in-law's flock, Moses led the animals to a place called Horeb (from a word meaning "desolate place," and another name for Sinai, 19:1,2; cf. Deut. 1:6). The exact location of Horeb (or Sinai) is unknown. Since early Christian times it has been identified as Jebel Musa in the southern Sinai peninsula. It also has been identified by some as nearby Jebel Serbal or Jebel Qaterin. Others have argued for its location in northwest Arabia in the vicinity of the Gulf of Aqaba or in the vicinity of Kadesh in the northern Sinai peninsula. At Horeb the angel of the Lord appeared to Moses in the midst of a scrubby desert plant that blazed furiously but was not consumed. The Hebrew word for "bush" (*seneh*) sounds much like Sinai and probably was intentionally chosen as a play on words.

For many years theologians have discussed the identity of the angel of the Lord. In some passages he seems to be different from God (Exod. 23:20-23; Num. 22:22; Judg. 5:23; 6:22; 2 Sam. 24:16; Zech. 1:12,13). In others the two are identical and interchangeable (Gen. 16:7-13, 22:11,12; 48:15,16; Exod. 3:2-4; Judg. 2:1; 6:11-24; 13:3-22). It seems best to understand the angel of the Lord as a visible manifestation of God Himself. These visible appearances of God in the Old Testament are called theophanies (from a word that means "an appearance of God"). They occur in the midst of natural phenomena (in fire, Exod. 3:2; in a cloud, Exod. 13:21; in a storm, Job 38:1; 1 Kings 19:11) or in human form (Exod. 33:21-23; Isa. 6:1; Gen. 18; Ezek. 1:26,27), but never in animal form. There are no theophanies in the New Testament because the ultimate theophany is found there — the incarnation of Jesus Christ.

God called Moses by name from the bush (a reassuring reminder that God deals with us as individuals), and Moses responded, "Here am I" (Hebrew literally, "Behold, me!"). His response is a formula that is found frequently in the Old Testament to express attentiveness to a summons and readiness to obey (cf. Abraham, Gen. 22:1; Samuel, 1 Sam. 3:4; Isaiah, Isa. 6:8). The command to Moses to remove his shoes in the desert wilderness is a reminder that wherever God is, that place is holy ground (cf. Joshua's experience, Josh. 5:15). In the ancient Near East it was a common practice for servants to remove their shoes in the presence of their master as an act of respect. Sandals still are removed as an expression of reverence in the East upon entering a mosque or sacred place.

God spoke to reassure Moses that he was not meeting an unknown God but the God of Abraham, Isaac, and Jacob. Moses hid his face in confusion and fear like Isaiah, who cried out, "Woe is me! for I am undone . . . for mine eyes have seen the King, the Lord of hosts" (Isa. 6:5), and like Ezekiel, who fell to the ground face down when he saw God (Ezek. 1:28). Moses knew that no one could see the face of God and live (Exod. 33:20; Judg. 13:22).

2. God's plan for deliverance (3:7-10)

God explained to Moses that He had not forgotten the affliction of His people. Exodus 3:7 marks the first time in the Old Testament that God used the term "my people." Later there would be times when in His anger God would say, "this people," but at Horeb He identified Himself with them and their sufferings. He was ready to bring them to a land that was occupied by Canaanites and other peoples, a land "flowing with milk and honey" (3:8; first use of this frequently-found expression in the Old Testament to describe Canaan; it symbolizes fertility and abundance). Then He announced that His plan for deliverance of His people included Moses as the deliverer. God works out His purposes

through human channels. He has a plan for every life. It had taken
eighty years for Moses to discover God's plan for his life, but God always
works out His purposes according to His timetable, not man's.

B. Excuses of a Reluctant Servant (3:11–4:12)

Up to this point Moses had probably rejoiced that God was about to
bring an end to His people's oppression, but when he learned that he
was to be their leader, he began to make his excuses. What follows is a
dialogue that is both humorous and painfully uncomfortable for the
reader. We see the humor in Moses' transparent attempts to excuse
himself, but we also are made uncomfortable because we see ourselves
and our excuses to avoid God's call all too clearly. A good title for what
follows would be "The Power of Negative Thinking!"

1. Not capable to do the task (3:11,12)

The brash self-confidence of Moses' youth was now gone. He did
not feel qualified for such an awesome responsibility. However, what
appears to be humility in his answers may really reveal a lack of faith in
God's ability or wisdom. His response to Moses, "I will be with thee,"
should have been enough (cf. Gen. 28:15; Josh. 1:5; Jer. 1:8; Hag. 1:13;
Matt. 28:20, where this same promise of God's presence is echoed). But
God further assured Moses that He had indeed called him by giving him
a sign: Moses would bring the liberated people back to worship God at
the very mountain where Moses was then standing. Such reassurance
should have been sufficient, but Moses had only begun his excuses.

2. No knowledge of God's name (3:13-22)

Moses' next excuse seemed reasonable enough. Supposing he did
accept the commission to go to Egypt, what would he tell the people if
they asked the name of the deity he claimed to represent? In ancient
times every deity had his own personal name; people believed it was
necessary to know his name in order to approach him in prayer or to ask
his help. The name also revealed something about the deity's attributes
and character. To know the name of the deity meant one enjoyed a
privileged relationship with that god. Moses' question may reflect his
own acceptance of these popular beliefs. It may also reveal his concern
that the Israelites in Egypt had forgotten the God of their fathers and
were worshiping the Egyptian deities (cf. Josh. 24:14 for clear evidence
that Israel did worship Egyptian deities and continued to worship them

even after they occupied the Promised Land).

Again God had an answer for Moses. He revealed to him His personal name, "I am." The meaning of this name has occupied the attention of Bible students for centuries. It is the name that identifies God as the covenant God of His people Israel. In the third person form in which it usually appears (rather than the first person, as here) it is spelled as YHWH, or JHVH. It appears without vowels because the Hebrew language was for centuries written without vowels. The pronunciation of words was transmitted orally from generation to generation. However, with the passing of time this particular name of God became so sacred that the people would not speak it. Therefore, the pronunciation was eventually forgotten, and today no one can be sure how it was actually pronounced. Most linguists believe that with vowels added the name Yahweh (or Jahveh). It usually is translated in English Bibles as "The Lord," and sometimes as "Jehovah."[1] The name comes from the Hebrew word "to be" and is clearly related to the self-existence of God. It has been understood to mean, "I am what I am," "I am because I am," "I will be what I will be," or "I cause to be" (i.e., "I bring into being" or "I am the one who creates"). YHWH is referred to also as the sacred Tetragrammation (from a Greek word that means "four letters").

However one interprets the name YHWH, the important fact to remember is that it was the living God speaking to Moses, and because He lived and spoke, victory was assured for His people. To settle whatever doubts lingered in Moses' mind about the responsiveness of the Israelites, God assured him that they would listen and that God Himself would smite Egypt until Pharaoh would be willing to let them leave the land.

3. People who will not believe (4:1-9)

Moses anticipated another difficulty. The people would not believe that God had appeared to him. Moses had every reason to expect the Israelites not to believe his words; unbelief in respect to the words of the prophets is found in every period of Israel's history (Ezek. 12:2; Acts 7:51,52). To meet this prospect God provided Moses with three signs

---

[1]The pronunciation "Jehovah" that began in medieval times grew out of a misunderstanding of the vowels of the name Adonai (Lord) written with the consonants JHVH by the Massoretes who supplied the vowels for the consonantal text around the sixth century A.D. This combination of vowels and consonants produces the hybrid "Jehovah" in English. However, the vowels were intended to instruct the reader to substitute the name "Adonai" for the sacred unpronounceable name.

that would surely convince the most skeptical: a rod (or shepherd's staff) that would become a serpent when cast to the ground; the hand that would become leprous when touched to the breast; and water from the Nile that would become blood when poured on the dry ground. A sign is an object or event whose meaning is not found within the sign itself but in the interpretation given to it; it reinforces the credibility of the one performing the sign. Signs frequently are mentioned in the Old Testament (e.g., Exod. 10:1; Num. 16:38; Deut. 4:34; 1 Sam. 14:10; Isa. 7:14).

Such remarkable demonstrations of power should have been sufficient to vanish any lingering doubts, but Moses had yet another excuse!

4. *Inability to speak eloquently* (4:10-12)

Moses did not believe that he was sufficiently fluent and eloquent to present his case convincingly to the Israelites so they would follow him (though he was having no difficulty making his own protests to God; cf. Acts 7:22, which describes Moses as "mighty in words"). He told God, "I am slow of speech" (literally, "heavy of mouth"). Again God had an answer for the reluctant prophet: "I will be with thy mouth, and teach thee what thou shalt say" (4:12). With God's assurance that the words he would need to speak would be given to him, Moses' last excuse was laid to rest. Now he had to be honest with God and admit that the real hindrance to his going was a rebellious spirit; he was unwilling to accept the call of God.

C. Moses' Refusal and God's Anger (4:13-17)

God had graciously and patiently dealt with each of Moses' objections. But now Moses had run out of excuses and it was time for him to admit, "If You won't accept my excuses, then I'll have to be honest. I don't want to go; send someone else!" At Moses' bold refusal, it is not surprising that God became angry. He did not relieve Moses of his responsibility but told him that his brother Aaron, identified as a Levite, would be the spokesman before the people. Nothing has been said previously about Aaron's existence or whereabouts; he probably lived in Egypt all the years that Moses was among the Midianites. Moses would still be the leader of the Israelites, and God would still speak directly to him and teach him what he should do. Moses then would repeat the words to Aaron, who in turn would proclaim them to the people. God's work would be done, and Moses was the one commissioned to do it.

However, by his disobedience, he forfeited the privilege of being the spokesman of God before the people.

Was Moses sincere in the excuses he made? He probably was as sincere as we are when we offer what seem to us valid, rational reasons for not doing what God wants us to do. This scene in which the greatest leader of the Hebrew people in the Old Testament revealed his own timorous faith should serve as encouragement that God does His work through imperfect, weak human beings, and not through perfected saints. Other great men of the Bible like Jacob, David, Elijah, and Jeremiah also had their moments of weakness and failure, yet God used all of them mightily.

For Further Study

1. In a Bible dictionary or encyclopedia (see bibliography) read articles on: theophany; angel of the Lord, names of God, signs.

2. What do you understand "a call from God" to mean?

3. Does every Christian receive a "call," or is the experience limited to a few, such as preachers, evangelists, missionaries, etc.?

4. What lessons can be learned from the excuses made by Moses?

5. Moses was eighty years old when God called him to lead the Israelites out of Egypt. Does God still have important work for older people to do?

Chapter 3

Preparations for Deliverance

(Exodus 4:18–7:7)

Momentous events in history often have obscure beginnings. An aged shepherd, a lonely spot in a desolate wasteland, a desert plant in flames, and the voice of God are the ingredients that are about to merge into a hitherto unheard of happening — a bold demand for freedom made to the mightiest ruler of the then-known world: "Let my people go!" It is a cry for recognition of human dignity that has echoed down to the present time.

A. Moses' Return to Egypt (4:18-31)

1. *Departure from Midian* (4:18-23)

God had already ordered Moses to go to Egypt, but he nevertheless went to his father-in-law to ask permission to depart. The normal rules of deference to the head of the family in the ancient Near East had to be observed, as Moses was still under Jethro's authority. He did not reveal to Jethro the real reason for his return, however, but only expressed a desire to visit his kinsmen in Egypt. God had already told him that those who had tried to kill him were now dead (4:19; cf. Matt. 2:20). Though only one son, Gershom, has previously been mentioned (2:22), we are told that Moses' wife and sons went with him. The second son, Eliezer, is not mentioned by name until later (18:4).

On the way God rehearsed with Moses what he was to do in Egypt. He told Moses to perform all the wonders ("miracles," RSV; *mophet,* Hebrew; displays of God's power that would attract attention and require explanation) that had been placed at his disposal and to demand the release of the Israelites from slavery. Then He added what must have been perplexing to Moses, even as it is to the modern reader: "I will harden his heart, that he shall not let the people go" (4:21). The statement is found eighteen times in the chapters that follow and is expressed three different ways: (1) God hardened Pharaoh's heart, 4:21; 7:3,13; 9:12; 10:1,20,27; 11:10; 14:4,8; (2) Pharaoh hardened his own heart, 8:15,32; 9:34; (3) and Pharaoh's heart was hardened, 7:14,22; 8:19; 9:7,35. Three different words are translated as "hardened" in these passages; one of them means "to be strong," hence stubborn (found in 4:21; 7:13,22; 8:19; 9:12,35; 10:20,27; 11:10; 14:4,8); the second means "to be heavy," hence dull or unresponsive (found in 7:14; 8:15,32; 9:7,34; 10:1); the third means "to be hard, severe," hence obstinate (found in 7:3). Together they describe Pharaoh's response to Moses' demands to free his people.

In Hebrew thought the heart was considered to be the seat of the intellect or will, not the emotions. Pharaoh's refusal to release the Israelites was an intellectual response, not an emotional one. But what does it mean that *"God* hardened Pharaoh's heart"? Does it imply that Pharaoh had no choice, even if he had desired to act otherwise? If so, how could he be punished for what he could not control? The solution to these vexing questions lies in the biblical paradox of the sovereignty of God set against the freedom of man. God's purposes will be accomplished, but man is free to accept or reject the will of God for his own life. Therefore, man is responsible and accountable for what he does. Whereas we would say, "The circumstances hardened Pharaoh's heart," there were no secondary causes for the ancient Hebrews. God was sovereign and all things could be traced to Him. Therefore, the Israelites could say, "Pharaoh hardened his heart," or "God hardened Pharaoh's heart," and see no difference or contradiction. As the same fire can melt wax or harden clay, so the same word of God can make one heart responsive and another hard and unresponsive. Ezekiel 20:8 adds the thought that Pharaoh was an instrument of God's punishment of Israel.

In speaking of Israel to Moses, God called the people "my son, even my firstborn" (4:22; the first mention of the "firstborn" theme that is so prominent in the Book of Exodus). In this statement Israel was brought into the closest, most loving and honored relationship that could be realized in the ancient Near East. The eldest son was given a place of special honor and respect. He received a double portion of the family inheritance (Deut. 21:17); the law of redemption applied to him in a special way (Exod. 13:11-15); and he was looked upon as the one who would succeed his father as head of the family or clan. He was given preferential status (Gen. 43:33), authority (Gen. 27:37), and responsibility (Gen. 37:22). As his birthright, he had claims on the family blessing (Gen. 27:1-4,35-37).

2. *Circumcision of Moses' son* (4:24-26)

Moses had accepted God's call, and he was on his way back to Egypt when without warning God sought to kill him (4:24). Zipporah acted quickly to circumcise her son (Gershom or Eliezer?) and hurled an accusation at her husband, "You are a bridegroom of blood to me" (4:25 RSV, NASB; "bloody husband," KJV). The whole episode is difficult to understand. Circumcision was widely practiced in the ancient Near East (the Philistines, Babylonians, and Assyrians did not practice it), but in Israel it took on the added significance of a sign of the covenant (Gen. 17:11). God "seeking to kill Moses" has been explained as a way of saying that Moses became dangerously ill or that he was being attacked by a desert demon, but it can best be understood as the consequence of Moses' neglect of circumcision for himself or his son. He could not lead the covenant people unless he himself was obedient to the requirements of the covenant. The episode underscores the tremendous importance of circumcision in ancient Israel. The Dutch philosopher Spinoza said that circumcision was the key to the separateness the Jewish people have maintained through the centuries.

3. *Israel's acceptance of Moses' leadership* (4:27-31)

God instructed Aaron (who must have been in Egypt at this time) to go out to the wilderness to meet his brother. Moses told Aaron what had happened and shared with him the role Aaron was to play. Together they returned to Goshen and gathered the people together to tell them what God was about to do. The people believed (4:31), as God had assured Moses they would. They did not raise the questions Moses had anticipated or show any reluctance to follow Moses — at least not yet!

B. First Confrontation With Pharaoh (5:1–6:13)

1. *Pharaoh's scorn* (5:1-9)

Soon after their return from the wilderness, Moses and Aaron were granted an audience with Pharaoh and abruptly demanded that he let the people go so they could hold a feast to God in the wilderness (5:1). Some have objected to the easy access to Pharaoh, but in that day if a person said, "I have a message from a deity," particularly if he had been raised in the court of Egypt and returned after a long absence, he would have been admitted. The word for "feast" (*hag*; a verbal form is used in 5:1) does not just mean a meal, but comes from a word, "to make a pilgrimage." The same word is in the Moslem vocabulary as *Hegira*, the flight of Mohammed from Mecca, and *Hadj*, the pilgrimage to Mecca a faithful Moslem hopes to make at least once in his life. Pharaoh clearly understood the demand to mean that the Israelites were not just asking time off for a weekend spiritual retreat!

The Egyptian pharaohs were considered by their people to be gods. Pharaoh's curt response to Moses was that of one god showing contempt for the challenge to his authority from another god whom he did not recognize: "Who is the LORD, that I should obey his voice to let Israel go? I know not the LORD, neither will I let Israel go" (5:2). The new ruler obviously had no more compassion for the Hebrew slaves than his predecessor and intended to continue the same oppressive policies. An ancient Egyptian papyrus reveals the inhumane attitude of the privileged classes toward the masses. In that document the rulers are quoted as saying about the slaves, "They have no hearts."

Pharaoh reacted to Moses' request for a three days' respite (or is a journey of three days' distance intended?) from their labors (5:3) by increasing their burdens. He accused them of being idle and instructed his taskmasters (Egyptians in charge of labor gangs) and foremen (Israelites who acted as immediate overseers of the workers) no longer to provide straw for them to make bricks. Henceforth, they would be required to produce the same number of bricks as before but with the added burden of going out and finding the straw. Pharaoh dismissed as a lie ("vain words," KJV) Moses' claim that his message was from the Lord (5:9).

2. The people's workload increased (5:10-14)

Instead of accomplishing the release of his people, Moses had brought greater trouble upon them. The people had to scour the land looking for straw for the bricks. When the quota was not forthcoming, the Israelite foremen were beaten by the Egyptian taskmasters. In Egypt bricks were made by soaking clay in water, mixing it with straw or other vegetable matter, shaping it by hand or with a wooden mold, and then drying it in the sun. Some of the great monuments of ancient Egypt that were made of sun-dried bricks still stand.

3. Complaints directed to Moses by the people (5:15-21)

The foremen complained bitterly to Pharaoh that they could not produce the bricks demanded without straw being provided, but he only repeated his accusation, "You are idle" (5:17). Finding no redress there, the foremen met Moses and Aaron and blamed them for their difficulties: "Ye have made our savour to be abhorred in the eyes of Pharaoh (5:21, KJV; "You have made us offensive in the sight of Pharaoh," RSV; the word "offensive" literally means "stink").

4. Complaints directed to God by Moses (5:22,23)

Moses could not understand why the burdens of his people increased. He had forgotten that God had told him their deliverance would not be easy (3:18,19) and accused God of bringing evil upon His people (5:22). Ascribing evil to God did not cause the Israelite the problem that it does for the modern theologian. For him God was sovereign; there were no secondary causes. Whatever happened, God did it (Amos 3:6; cf. 1 Sam. 16:14; 1 Kings 22:20,21; Isa. 45:7; Jer. 20:7; Ezek. 14:9). We would say, "Why did God *permit* the evil to happen?" Moses said, "Why did you *do* this evil?" If we subscribe to belief in the absolute sovereignty of God, then we are forced to say that there could be no evil in the world unless God permitted it to exist. However, this does not force us to conclude that God is the author of sin and evil. Sin and evil find their origin in man, who was created with the freedom to choose or reject God. In our insistence upon emphasizing the freedom of man to reject God, we often forget that man also has the freedom to accept God. In order for the creature's love to be freely given to God, God took the risk of losing him altogether. For the moment Moses found himself in the same dilemma of modern man: when the sting of evil touches us and we do not understand why, we may find ourselves lashing out at God. Moses accused God; he should have pointed the accusing finger at the cruel pharaoh, indifferent to human misery.

5. God's assurance of victory (6:1-13)

God calmed the distraught Moses with the assurance that he would soon see God at work against Pharaoh. He brought to Moses' remembrance the new name He had revealed to him at Sinai, "the Lord" (6:3; "Jehovah," KJV; cf. 3:13,14). The patriarchs, Abraham, Isaac, and Jacob, had not been privileged to know the personal name of God; they had called Him God Almighty (Hebrew, *El Shaddai*, taken by some to mean "God of the mountains" and by others as "God of devastating power").

He reaffirmed His promise to free the people from their bondage (6:6) with the words, "I will deliver you" (a word that can be used of delivering the prey from the mouth of a wild animal [Amos 3:12], but usually of deliverance from one's enemies or from difficulties), and "I will redeem you" (a term used frequently in the Old Testament to describe the duties of the next of kin to right wrongs done to a member of his family or help in time of distress; God was going to be Israel's kinsman). The people would know that He was their God by what He did for them (6:7).

Moses repeated God's reassuring words of victory to the oppressed Israelites, but they would not believe him "for anguish of spirit and for cruel bondage" (6:9). Sometimes Christians find their sufferings and trials to be so intense, like the Israelites, that they cannot hear or believe the unchanging promises of God. The Israelites' discouragement seemed to infect Moses. When God told him to return to Pharaoh with His demand to release the people, Moses responded that if the Israelites would not listen to him, he could not expect Pharaoh to listen. He resorted to an earlier excuse (4:10) that he was not eloquent, "[I] am a man of uncircumcised lips" (6:12; that is, closed in, unable to speak fluently; the expression is used elsewhere of the heart, Lev. 26:41; Jer. 9:26; and the ear, Jer. 6:10). God's only response was to repeat His command that the people of Israel be brought out of the land of Egypt (6:13).

C. Parenthetical (6:14–7:7)

1. *The genealogy of Moses and Aaron* (6:14-27)

There is a break in the narrative after verse 13. The story picks up again at verse 28. A genealogy is inserted between these verses to establish the lineage of Moses and Aaron. It includes the descendants of Reuben, Simeon, and Levi, but shows no interest in the other sons of Jacob and their descendants. Its attention is focused upon Aaron and his descendants, who would exercise the role of priests in the covenant nation that was in the process of being formed. It is this genealogy that reveals the names of the parents of Aaron and Moses (6:20), a detail that was omitted earlier (2:1,2). Korah, who will figure prominently later in a rebellion that brought disaster to him and his family (Num. 16:1-50), is included in the genealogy as a son of Izhar, the brother of Moses' father Amram. Another name of interest is Putiel (6:25), father-in-law of Aaron's son and successor as high priest, Eleazer (Num. 20:25-28). Putiel is a name partly of Egyptian derivation combined with the He-

brew "El" (one of the names of God in the Old Testament). It suggests
that intermarriage with Egyptians probably took place during the Israelites' sojourn in Egypt.

2. *The call of Moses retold* (6:28–7:7)

These verses do not add anything new to the story except to tell us
that Moses was eighty and Aaron eighty-three when they spoke to
Pharaoh (7:7). The Bible divides the life of Moses into three equal
periods of forty years (Acts 7:23; Exod. 7:7; Deut. 34:7). Dwight L.
Moody has been quoted as saying that "Moses spent forty years in
Pharaoh's court thinking he was somebody, forty years in the desert
learning that he was nobody, and forty years showing what God can do
with a somebody who found out he was a nobody."

For Further Study

1. In a Bible dictionary or encyclopedia (see bibliography) read
articles on: circumcision, brickmaking, genealogy, names of God (God
Almighty).

2. Can you reconcile the sovereignty of God and the freedom of
man? What are some implications of these biblical doctrines for us?

3. What useful purpose can defeats and setbacks serve?

4. As Christians we do not doubt that God acts and works out His
purposes. Our problem is with His timetable. Recall a time when God
did not act when you expected and what you learned from the experience.

5. Do you agree that all the misery and suffering in the world are
due to man, not God? What about hunger, floods, tornadoes, disease?

Chapter 4

The Confrontation With Pharaoh

(Exodus 7:8–11:10)

Two aged men pitted against all the power of Egypt seemed destined for failure. The odds appeared to be overwhelmingly against them except for one factor, and that was God. God was on the side of Moses and Aaron, and Pharaoh was going to learn that two plus God equals enough. "If God is for us, who can be against us?" (Rom. 8:31, NIV).

A. Signs of Power Given to Moses (7:8-13)

Earlier God had given three signs to Moses to remove the unbelief of the Israelites who might question whether God had really appeared to him (4:1-9). One of these signs was a rod that turned to a serpent when thrown to the ground. The same sign was about to be used again, this time for the benefit of an unbelieving pharaoh. God told Moses that Pharaoh would demand that he perform a miracle (7:9; *mophet*, the same word found in 4:21) to prove he was speaking for God. The establishing of one's legitimacy through the working of a sign was common in the ancient world. God told Moses to have Aaron throw his rod to the ground and it would turn to a serpent. The word for serpent in 4:3 and 7:15 *(nahash)* is different from the word found in 7:9,10,12 *(tannin)*. *Nahash* is the usual word for serpent or snake, whereas *tannin* is a word used of large reptiles or sea monsters (some think "crocodile" would be a proper translation of *tannin* in this passage). As both words are found in the same context of chapter 7, the best explanation (apart from a documentary hypothesis that says two different literary sources were incorporated) is that the words came to be used interchangeably.

Moses and Aaron went to Pharaoh and threw the rod down before the Egyptian ruler as God had commanded. The rod became a serpent, but Pharaoh, apparently unimpressed, called his own magicians (a

Jewish tradition says the magicians were named Jannes and Jambres; they are mentioned in 2 Tim. 3:8), and they did the same thing through their secret arts. We are not told exactly how they duplicated the feat, but magical arts were highly developed in ancient Egypt. The magicians' performance has been explained as an example of the art of serpent charming that is still practiced in the East today. Cobras are paralyzed by putting pressure on a nerve in their neck, and when they are thrown to the ground the jolt causes them to recover and slither away. This rational explanation of "rabbit-from-the-hat" magic has been rejected by those who believe a genuine conflict of power was taking place between the God of Israel and the forces of evil. It is true that evil forces can make a reasonable facsimile of God's work that could deceive the very elect if possible (Matt. 24:24). Whichever explanation is correct, the magicians did not enjoy their triumph for long, for Aaron's rod swallowed up their rods. But even this demonstration of superior power did not convince Pharaoh. His heart was hardened, and he refused to listen to them (7:13).

B. The Plagues (7:14–11:10)

The contest between Moses and Pharaoh was ready to begin in earnest. Moses was about to unleash a series of ten plagues upon Egypt that would not leave a single Egyptian household untouched and would cause Pharaoh to cry out to the Israelites to get out of his country (12:32).

Before examining each of the plagues, some general observations are in order. The number of plagues was ten, a number of completeness in biblical numerology. Attempts have been made to discover some kind of organizing principle for the first nine plagues in groups of three (see Keil and Delitzsch). The first three are characterized by some scholars by their loathesome nature, the second three by physical pain, and the final trio by natural phenomena. However, such efforts prove unsatisfactory, as the arbitrary distinctions cannot be maintained (would flies be any less loathsome than frogs?). Attempts have been made to see progression in the severity of the plagues, but except for the tenth, this is difficult to demonstrate (how is darkness more severe than boils?). Attempts have been made to demonstrate that each plague was directed against an Egyptian deity[1]; this approach does have some merit.

We are more certain of agreement concerning the pattern that characterized the contest between Moses and Pharaoh. Though every

---

[1] Bernard L. Ramm, *Let My People Go* (Glendale, Cal.: G/L Publications, 1974), p. 61.

element is not present in all of the plagues, a common pattern is apparent: first, the request, "Let my people go"; the Hebrew is not quite as polite as the English translation; it is an emphatic imperative of the verb *shalach* and could be translated, "Send my people away!" Then upon Pharaoh's refusal to accede to the demand, a plague is threatened. This is followed by Pharaoh's response (either acceptance and later change of mind, an offer of compromise, or outright rejection). We cannot be sure how much time elapsed during the contest, but it may have been as much as six months.

The most important question that can be raised is, "How shall the plagues be interpreted?" Are they to be explained as a later fabrication (an etiological story created years later to explain how the Israelites were able to leave Egypt)? Are they to be taken as symbolical rather than historical? Should they be explained as natural phenomena that still can be observed in Egypt today? Or can they be accepted as the Bible presents them — as miraculous demonstrations of the power of God?

The question of the miraculous (or thaumaturgy, the performance of miracles or wonders) in the Bible must be taken seriously. To "explain away" or excise one miracle will not solve the problem. The Bible is filled with miraculous tales, and the removal of one requires the removal of all. The real problem does not seem to be whether the miracles actually happened, but whether in a scientifically-oriented age man has shut himself off from belief in the supernatural. People respond to miracles in different ways. One response to the miraculous is that of outright rejection because of unbelief in the supernatural. A second response is to find natural explanations that do not really deny the existence of God, but at the same time remove Him from the scene (for example, Jesus walking on the water becomes an optical illusion created by His nearness to the water as He walked along the shore by the water's edge).[2]

A third response to miracles is to understand that they are seen only through eyes of faith. Two people observing the same thing happening will "see" it differently. Through eyes of unbelief the activity of God in the event must be denied or else the beholder would be forced to believe, so he finds a rational explanation that satisfies him. Eyes of faith observe the same event but have no difficulty in seeing God at work. For example, a person of faith believes God has the power to separate the

---

[2]For detailed "natural" explanations of the ten plagues, see Dewey M. Beegle, *Moses, the Servant of Yahweh* (Grand Rapids: William B. Eerdmans Publishing Co., 1972) and Jack Finegan, *Let My People Go* (New York: Harper and Row, 1963).

waters of the sea to allow the children of Israel to pass through; unbelief proposes a coincidental landslide upstream that blocked the waters. Faith believes Lazarus was really raised from the dead; unbelief says his friends hid him in the tomb and brought him forth at the proper moment to convince the people that Jesus was really a wonder-worker. Dostoevsky in *The Brothers Karamazov* correctly observed that when man rejects miracles, he rejects God. The real essence of miracle, then, is the acknowledgment that God is at work.

One other observation must be made concerning the plagues inflicted upon the Egyptians. The frogs, gnats, flies, hail, locusts, darkness, etc., that the Egyptians experienced were real, not hallucinatory. They were not phenomena that had never previously been observed or existed. Wherein, then, lay the miracle? The plagues must be acknowledged as miracles because of the timing (they occurred when Moses said they would), the intensity (the severity of the frogs, hail, darkness, etc., had not previously been experienced), and location (they occurred where Pharaoh and the Egyptians would experience them, not a hundred miles away). All these factors affirm God's control of the plagues. If the plagues were only "natural" phenomena that had frequently been experienced in Egypt, they would not have resulted in the deliverance of the Israelites.

1. *Water changes to blood* (7:14-25)

God instructed Moses to go out to the Nile River in the morning to meet Pharaoh, who may have been there to bathe, to offer his devotions to the Nile, or to see if the river was beginning to rise to signal the beginning of the flood season. There he was to demand that Pharaoh release the Israelites to serve God in the wilderness (7:16). To convince Pharaoh that the Lord was responsible for the demand, Moses was told to strike the Nile with a rod (the one that had turned into a serpent, 7:9,10). The water would be turned to blood, killing all the fish (an important source of food for the Egyptians) in the river and making its water unfit to drink. Even water in canals and storage vessels would be changed to blood. It is significant that because the Nile was considered to be a deity, the first plague probably was interpreted by the Egyptians as a frontal assault on the gods of Egypt.

Moses carried out the instructions and the water did change to blood, but the Egyptian magicians were able to duplicate the same thing with their magical arts (though they might have been more helpful by turning the blood back to water). The people were forced to dig shallow wells in the soil adjoining the Nile to find potable water. Pharaoh, however, remained unimpressed and would not listen to Moses.

The two branches of the Nile, the White Nile (whose source is in the lake country of east-central Africa near the equator) and the Blue Nile (whose source is in the mountains of Ethiopia), join together at Khartoum and flow toward the Mediterranean, fed by another tributary north of Khartoum, the Atbara, whose source is also in the highlands of Ethiopia. During flood season a large amount of the red soil of the Ethiopian plateau is washed down into the Blue Nile and the Atbara, giving them a reddish color that could easily be compared to blood (the argument being that blood in the Bible is not always literal blood; cf. Joel 2:31). This explanation alone, however, would not explain the death of the fish. A German botanist, Gessner, has proposed that mountain algae, known as flagellates, and their bacteria entered the water and caused the death of the fish and the stench of the water that would have made it unfit for drinking. These are scientific explanations that have been proposed to account for the first plague. Faith could accept these explanations if at the same time it is acknowledged that God was directing the forces of nature to bring about Israel's liberation. Apparently Pharaoh was able to convince himself that the plague could be explained as a "natural" phenomenon, for his heart remained hardened, and he would not listen to Moses and Aaron.

2. Frogs fill the land (8:1-15)

Seven days later God told Moses to return to Pharaoh with the same demand, "Let my people go." If he would not, a plague of frogs would be loosed upon the land that would fill the Nile, enter the houses, ovens, kneading bowls, and the beds of Pharaoh and all his people. The frog was associated with the goddess Heqt, who assisted women at childbirth and so was a symbol of life-giving power to the Egyptians. The second plague may, therefore, have been interpreted as another attack upon the power of the Egyptian deities. The Lord ordered Aaron to stretch out his hand with the rod over the rivers, canals, and pools, and to cause frogs to cover the land of Egypt. The magicians were able to do the same thing by their magical arts to demonstrate that the frogs were not a special sign from Moses' God. It is uncertain how they were helping Pharaoh by producing more frogs; if they really had power, they could have been more helpful by removing the frogs!

This time, however, Pharaoh was sufficiently impressed to appeal to Moses to remove the frogs, and he agreed to let the people go to sacrifice to the Lord. Moses asked Pharaoh to designate the time for the removal of the frogs so that the ruler would be convinced that there was no one like the God of the Israelites. By setting the time, he would know that the death of the frogs did not happen by chance. The beleaguered pharaoh asked for the removal of the frogs the next day. Moses and Aaron departed from the king, and Moses asked the Lord to remove the frogs in accordance with the agreement with Pharaoh. God heard Moses, and the frogs died in the houses, courtyards, and in the fields. The Egyptians gathered them in great piles, and the land was filled with their odor. But when Pharaoh saw there was a respite (Hebrew, "an open space"), he hardened his heart and refused to keep his agreement. The impressions made upon him by the first two afflictions wore off quickly; he was not yet convinced of the power of God.

Those who prefer a "natural" explanation (as Pharaoh must have) suggest that the mass of dead fish in the Nile (7:21) drove the frogs (common in Egypt, particularly after the flooding of the Nile) to the land where they entered houses and fields to find water and shelter from the sun. Further, the phenomenon of dead fish suggests that they were infected with a bacillus that spread to the frogs and would explain their sudden death and rapid decomposition.

3. Gnats cover man and beast (8:16-19)

When Pharaoh refused to yield in face of the first two plagues, God ordered Moses to have Aaron strike the dust of the earth so that it would become gnats throughout Egypt. The exact identity of the insect is uncertain; the Hebrew word (kinnim) occurs only here, Exodus 8:16-18, and in Psalm 105:31 (also Isa. 51:6, "gnats," RSV; but translated "in like manner," KJV), and refers to some kind of small insect. The KJV translates it as "lice," but they are not characteristically found in Egypt. The word also has been translated as gnats, mosquitoes, fleas, sand flies, maggots, and gadflies. Whatever the precise identity of the insect, it filled the land when Aaron struck the dust and covered people and animals. When the magicians were unable to reproduce the phenomenon by their magical arts, they acknowledged to Pharaoh, "This is the finger of God." Perhaps they recognized what Pharaoh was yet unwilling to admit — that God had permitted their counterfeiting earlier, but would no longer. The expression, "finger of God," is a symbol of divine power (cf. Luke 11:20). The law given to Moses was written by "the finger of God" (Exod. 31:18; Deut. 9:10). However, Pharaoh's heart remained hardened; he was as obstinate as ever and would not listen to the appeals of his own magicians (8:19).

4. Flies swarm throughout the land (8:20-32)

The third plague had failed to convince Pharaoh, but there was to be no respite. God instructed Moses to rise early and meet Pharaoh on his way to the river and repeat his demand, "Let my people go, that they may serve me." If Pharaoh would not acquiesce, swarms of flies would be sent that would cover the king, his servants, the people, their houses, and even the ground on which they stood. The fly was so common in Egypt that it was used as a symbol of the nation in Isaiah 7:18 and 18:1. This plague, however, would be different. God told Moses that the land of Goshen (first mentioned in Exodus by name in v. 22; located in the Wadi Tumilat of the northeastern delta region) would be set apart so that no flies would swarm there in order to convince Pharaoh that God really was in control. Pharaoh was given only one day to decide, and when he refused to yield, the land was filled with swarms of flies. This was sufficient to cause Pharaoh to offer his first concession: "Go ye, sacrifice to your God in the land" (8:25). Moses had asked permission for the people to go into the wilderness, but Pharaoh did not want them to go too far away so that he could keep an eye on them. Moses rejected the concession on the grounds that if the Egyptians saw the Israelites offering animal sacrifices, they would be incensed and stone the Israelites.

Animal sacrifice was not completely unknown in Egypt, but the Egyptians deemed it unlawful to sacrifice some animals, such as the cow (sacred to Isis), the bull, sheep, and goats. They preferred vegetable offerings along with poultry and pieces of meat. Moses' answer to Pharaoh should perhaps be interpreted to mean that up to that time the Israelites had neglected to offer sacrifices to God since settling in Egypt. Their acceptance of Egyptian religious practices during the sojourn there was verified later by Joshua (Josh. 24:14,23).

With the rejection of the first compromise, Pharaoh proposed a second: he would let the people go into the wilderness out of sight of the Egyptians to sacrifice, "only you shall not go very far away" (8:28). Moses was willing to accept the second concession. He agreed to pray for the removal of the flies but warned Pharaoh as he departed not to change his mind. But as soon as the flies disappeared, Pharaoh hardened his heart again and would not let the people go.

5. *Disease inflicts the animals* (9:1-7)

God told Moses to return to Pharaoh with his same demand, "Let my people go." This time the demand was accompanied by the threat of a severe plague (9:3, "grievous murrain," KJV; the Hebrew, *deber*, is a general word for pestilence or plague) upon all the animals of Egypt — cattle, horses, donkeys, camels, herds, and flocks. Again the Israelites would be protected from the plague; none of their animals would die. The exact nature of the plague cannot be determined, but it frequently has been identified as anthrax, a highly contagious and usually fatal disease. The plague struck the animals the day after Moses spoke to Pharaoh, but even though he was informed that none of the Israelite animals died, he was not swayed and would not allow the Israelites to go.

6. *Boils break out on man and beast* (9:8-12)

There was to be no letup in the afflictions upon the stubborn Pharaoh. God ordered Moses to take handfuls of ashes from the kiln (used for baking pottery, burning lime, or making charcoal) and scatter them toward heaven in the sight of Pharaoh. The ashes would become fine dust and cover the land, producing boils (9:9; the same word used to describe the sickness of Hezekiah, 2 Kings 20:7, and of Job, 2:7) that would break out in sores upon people and animals alike. The command was carried out. Even the magicians were unable to prevent the boils from afflicting their own bodies, and they appealed to Pharaoh, but he would not listen to them. Some scholars have noted that the description of the boils fits anthrax closely and could be the same disease that killed the frogs and the cattle earlier.

7. *Hail shatters the land* (9:13-35)

Then God ordered Moses to rise early the next day and go to Pharaoh and repeat his demand to let the people go, upon threat of a severe hail, such as had never been seen in Egypt, that would destroy every person and animal that did not seek shelter. This plague was different from previous plagues because the people could save themselves this time if they would; it would be a test of the Egyptians' belief in God. God further instructed Moses to tell Pharaoh that He could already have destroyed all of them, but He had let them live to show His power and so that His name would be declared throughout all the earth (9:15,16). Some of Pharaoh's attendants believed Moses' threat and sought shelter for themselves, their slaves, and cattle that were in the field. When it struck, the hail shattered the land of Egypt, destroying everything that was in the open — people, cattle, plants, and trees. By contrast, there was no hail in Goshen, where the Israelites were.

In view of the statement in 9:6 that all the cattle of the Egyptians died as a result of the disease that struck them, an explanation is needed to account for the cattle that still remained when the hail struck (9:19). Most commentators agree that the solution is not difficult to find; 9:3 makes it clear that only cattle in the field were affected by the disease, so there is no real inconsistency in the narrative.

When Pharaoh saw the terrible havoc wrought by the hail, he called for Moses and Aaron and made what must have been for him an extremely difficult confession, "I have sinned this time: the LORD is righteous, and I and my people are wicked" (9:27). He appealed to Moses to stop the hail with the promise that he would let the Israelites go immediately. Moses agreed to this but told Pharaoh that he knew the stubborn ruler and his servants did not yet fear the Lord God (9:30). Even as Moses expected, as soon as the hail ceased, Pharaoh hardened his heart and would not let the people go. Pharaoh was like others who have been anxious for deliverance from their difficulties and have made vows to God, "Lord, if you will get me out of this situation, I will do thus-and-so for You." But when the affliction is removed, they quickly forget their vows.

8. *Locusts cover the land* (10:1-20)

Before God sent Moses back to Pharaoh to announce the next plague, He told him that the heart of Pharaoh and his servants had been hardened so that God could perform His signs among them, and future generations of Israelite parents would tell their children how God had triumphed over the Egyptians (10:2). Previously God had said that the plagues were brought on Egypt so that the Egyptians would know that He was the Lord (7:5), but now He says that the purpose of the plagues is so that the Israelites may know that He is the Lord (10:2).

Moses and Aaron returned to Pharaoh to announce the eighth plague — locusts that would cover the land so that no one would be able to see the ground. They would eat everything that had not been destroyed by the hail and would fill the houses of the Egyptians. Even

Pharaoh's attendants by now were convinced. For the first time they pleaded with the monarch to release the Israelites, whose presence was bringing about the ruin of Egypt. Pharaoh was swayed by the frantic appeals of his courtiers and recalled Moses and Aaron, and for the first time attempted to negotiate with Moses before another plague struck. He agreed to let the Israelites go but wanted to know who would make the trip. Moses answered that all of them would go — young, old, children, and their livestock. With bitter sarcasm Pharaoh accused Moses of evil intents (10:10). He offered to let the men go but insisted that the families and possessions remain as a guarantee that the others would return. After making the concession begrudgingly, Pharaoh drove Moses and Aaron from his presence (10:11).

The compromise was unacceptable, and God ordered Moses to stretch his rod over the land of Egypt to initiate the plague of locusts. An east wind began blowing that brought the locusts to the land by the next day. They swarmed over the ground, devouring all the plants and fruit of the trees that had escaped the hail, leaving no vegetation or even a sprig of greenery anywhere. The destruction brought Pharaoh again to the place where he admitted to Moses and Aaron that he had sinned against the Lord their God and against them (10:17). This time he did not include the people in the blame (cf. 9:27) but took all the responsibility upon himself. Moses left Pharaoh's presence and prayed to the Lord for the removal of the locusts. Soon a strong west wind arose and carried all the locusts away and drove them into the Red Sea (that is, Sea of Reeds; see discussion at 13:18); not a locust was left in Egypt. But again Pharaoh changed his mind and refused to let the Israelites go.

Locusts still are one of the most feared catastrophes in the Near East. They descend upon a land like a black cloud, so dense that sometimes they produce temporary darkness over the land. They quickly destroy everything edible in sight with insatiable appetites, leaving behind ruin and famine. It has been documented that in 1889 a swarm of locusts crossing the Red Sea was estimated to cover an area of 2000 square miles. In 1881, in Cyprus, 1300 tons of locust eggs were destroyed. An invasion of locusts in Joppa in 1865 covered the ground for miles around to a height of several inches. Locust swarms have been sighted 1200 miles at sea.

9. *Darkness envelops the land* (10:21-29)

There were yet two plagues remaining in store for Pharaoh and the

Egyptians. God ordered Moses to bring darkness upon the land, darkness so oppressive that it would be felt. The darkness lasted for three days; it was so thick people could not see one another and dared not go abroad into the streets or fields. But the darkness did not come to the Israelites in Goshen, as further proof for Pharaoh that Moses' God was responsible for the plagues. A harried Pharaoh once again was reduced to making concessions to the Israelites. He agreed to let them go and worship God, taking their families with them, but he insisted that they leave their flocks and herds behind. Thus he felt assured that the Israelites would return. Moses refused to accept the concession and insisted that they take all their livestock so that they would have animals available for sacrifices. Moses' intransigence angered Pharaoh, and he ordered Moses out of his presence with the threat that if he ever saw him again, Moses would be put to death. Whatever verbal sparring had taken place previously, it was clear to both Pharaoh and Moses by now that the issue at stake was the complete liberation of the children of Israel.

The darkness in Egypt has been explained as a *khamsin*, a hot wind from the desert that contains an immense quantity of sand and blows into Egypt in the spring of the year, usually lasting two or three days. The resulting sandstorm is so heavy that the atmosphere grows dark and the sun is blotted out from view. However, unless there had been something unique about the darkness, it would not have caused such fear among the Egyptians or caused Pharaoh to propose his concession. Most peoples of the ancient Near East considered darkness to be the realm of evil spirits and chaos. A darkness that lasted for three days might have made them believe the forces of darkness had triumphed. The irony of the ninth plague may be that it was directed against the power of Re, the sun god and a chief Egyptian deity.

10. *Death announced for the firstborn* (11:1-10)

There remained in store for Egypt one more plague (11:1, literally, a stroke or blow; a different word from that used in 9:3), and this one would bring about the release of the Israelites where the others had failed. God told Moses to instruct the Israelites to go to the Egyptians and ask (11:2; "borrow," KJV, but this translation creates an ethical dilemma that would have the Israelites getting the goods of the Egyptians through deceit; the Hebrew word, however, means "to ask") for their jewelry of silver and gold. The willingness of the Egyptians to part with their valuables can be explained as fear (they had experienced the terrible plagues that had not harmed the Israelites) and guilt (they knew the Israelites had been mistreated and underpaid, and they were attempting to make reparations in hope of placating the Israelite deity).

Moses told Pharaoh that at midnight the Lord would go through the land, bringing death to every firstborn in the land, from the firstborn of Pharaoh to the firstborn of the lowliest servant and the firstborn of the animals (11:5). Since Pharaoh was looked upon as a god, if he could not protect his firstborn (who in turn would be made a god-king), his impotence would be exposed. There would be an outcry of panic such as had never been known in Egypt, but all would be so quiet and peaceful in Goshen that not a dog would growl (11:7; Hebrew literally, "sharpen its tongue") that night. The Israelites had cried to God (2:23) and to Pharaoh (5:15), but now it was the Egyptians' turn to cry out in anguish at God's judgment on them. Moses warned Pharaoh as he turned and left in anger that the ruler's arrogant stubbornness would soon bring the Egyptians to Moses to plead with him to take his people out of their country.

As the series of plagues draw to an end, the question might be asked, "Why was more than one plague necessary?" One answer is that they affirm the longsuffering of God. He gave sufficient opportunity for Pharaoh to avoid the plague of death on the land. He could have believed God and spared the Egyptians the suffering that struck them. Another explanation is that Pharaoh needed convincing that it was really God at work. One plague or two could always have been explained as "coincidence," but ten should have convinced even the most skeptical that it was the hand of God that was responsible for the series of calamities.

In response to a second question, "What was the real purpose of the plagues?" the answer is threefold: (1) To deliver Israel from Egyptian bondage (7:4); (2) to make Egypt know that Yahweh was truly God (7:5, 17; 8:22); (3) and to punish the Egyptians for their sins (9:27, 34). An objection might be raised to the last answer that it was Pharaoh who sinned, and the Egyptians were innocent bystanders to the contest that swirled about them. However, the Egyptians had passively stood by and watched the enslavement and mistreatment of the Israelites and therefore shared in the responsibility for their oppression. Passiveness or failure to protest injustice sometimes can be just as great a sin as sin actively committed.

For Further Study

1. In a Bible dictionary or encyclopedia (see bibliography) read articles on: plagues, Nile River, magicians, locusts.

2. Was it right for the people of Egypt to be afflicted because of the stubborn refusal of Pharaoh to release the Israelites?

3. Study again the compromises Pharaoh proposed to Moses during the series of plagues (8:25,28; 10:11,24). What are some lessons that can be learned from these compromises proposed by Pharaoh?

4. What is your understanding of a miracle?

5. Why did Pharaoh require so much convincing to believe that God was responsible for the plagues that were afflicting Egypt?

PART TWO: DELIVERANCE FROM EGYPT

Chapter 5

The Passover and Departure From Egypt

(Exodus 12:1–15:21)

Nine plagues already had been inflicted upon Egypt, and still the obstinate Pharaoh persisted in his refusal to let the Israelites leave Egypt. One more plague was about to be experienced, the visitation of death upon the firstborn of man and animal in every household in Egypt. This plague would succeed where the others had failed. It would be known by the Jewish people from that night forward as the Passover (*Pesach* in Hebrew; its meaning is uncertain, perhaps from a word, "leap," "limp," or "protect"; the word has come into English, through Greek, as "paschal"). It would be remembered as a "night different from all other nights of the year," when God delivered His people from Egyptian bondage, the first "Independence Day" in history.

A. Institution of the Passover (12:1-36)

1. *Instructions for the first Passover* (12:1-13)

God announced to Moses and Aaron that the tenth plague would strike Egypt on the fourteenth day of the month (the month of Abib in Hebrew, later known as Nisan, corresponding to our March-April). The Israelites were to begin preparations to protect themselves from the plague on the tenth day of that month, which would thereafter be considered the first month of the new year (12:2,3). Passover, therefore, was both a spring festival and a new year festival. In the ancient Near East the Babylonian New Year was observed in the spring, but in Canaan it occurred in the fall. Some scholars believe that Israel followed the Canaanite method of reckoning before the Exile but changed to the Babylonian calendar after the Exile. Others believe that the Israelites observed both civil and religious new years (civil in the fall and religious in the spring). Today Passover is observed in the spring and New Year (Rosh Hashanah) in the fall.

Moses and Aaron were instructed to tell the congregation (12:3; first occurrence of the word that would become the technical term for Israel as an organized religious community) to take a lamb for each household. The word for "lamb" is *seh,* which can be either a sheep or goat (cf. 12:5). If the household was too small to eat an entire animal, then next door neighbors would share the same lamb. A later regulation fixed ten as the number of persons for each lamb. Passover was instituted as a family observance, and it still is celebrated in the home. The lamb could not be just any lamb; it had to be without blemish, male, and one year old. It had to be separated from the flock on the tenth of the month and kept till the fourteenth when it would be killed in the evening (literally, "between the two evenings," interpreted by the Talmud as the time between sunset and the appearance of the first stars). Some of the blood was to be put on the two door posts and the lintel of the houses in which the lambs were eaten. The doorway was regarded in ancient times as the most sacred part of the house and therefore required special protection.

The meat was to be roasted whole, along with the head and intestines. It was never eaten raw, lest blood be consumed. Also, it could not be boiled with water (Deut. 16:7 represents a later change with its demand to boil the meat). It then was eaten with unleavened bread and bitter herbs. The significance of bitter herbs is not explained here, but later they would be used to remind the Israelites of their bitter experiences as slaves. The Mishnah lists five herbs that could be eaten: lettuce, chicory, pepperwort, snakeroot, and dandelion. None of the meat was to be left until morning; whatever remained was to be burned. The people were to eat hastily, being fully clothed with sandals on their feet and a staff in their hands.

While the Israelites were shut up inside their houses, protected by the mark of blood on their doors, God would pass through the land and kill (Hebrew, "smite," but the word usually means "kill") all the firstborn of man and animal, passing over only those houses identified by the protecting mark of blood. (See also Gen. 4:15; Ezek. 9:4; Rev. 7:3 for other examples of marks of divine protection.) The New Testament interprets the act of smearing blood on the door as evidence of faith (Heb. 11:28). God declared that He was about to execute judgments on the gods of Egypt (12:12). He further promised that the plague (Hebrew, *negeph,* a blow or striking) would not fall upon the Israelites.

2. *Instructions for the Feast of Unleavened Bread* (12:14-20)

In addition to eating the Passover lamb, the Israelites were instructed to eat only unleavened bread (Hebrew, *maṣṣot*, popularly called today matzah bread) for seven days; all leaven was to be carefully removed from the house (12:15). Leaven is a substance added to dough to produce fermentation. The word is used also to designate the fermented dough, a portion of which was reserved from the previous day's baking to be used for leavening in the next batch of dough. Leaven eventually became a symbol of corruption and impurity and was compared to the pervasive spread of sin (cf. Matt. 16:6; 1 Cor. 5:6-8; Gal. 5:9).

Many Old Testament scholars believe that originally Passover and the Feast of Unleavened Bread were two separate feasts. They find the antecedents of the Passover in the sacrifices offered by nomadic herdsmen when they moved to a new place in the spring from their winter grazing grounds; the purpose of their sacrifices was to keep away evil spirits and other unknown dangers. These same scholars believe that the Feast of Unleavened Bread was of Canaanite origin and was celebrated on the occasion of barley harvest to mark the separation between the bread of the old crop of grain and the bread of the new crop, and that the two separate feasts were eventually merged and celebrated together after Israel settled in Canaan. Though it is true that the festivals do find parallels elsewhere in ancient Near Eastern cultures, their distinctiveness lies in the new meaning given to them to commemorate the Exodus. Other examples of practices that were given new meaning in the Bible are circumcision, widely practiced in the ancient Near East, which became a symbol of the covenant relation between God and Abraham (Gen. 17:9-14), and the cross, an instrument of execution in Roman times that became the symbol of the Christian faith.

The Israelite who ate leavened bread during the seven days would be "cut off from Israel" (12:15), that is, excommunicated from the community in which he lived. Expulsion from the tribal community could be fatal in ancient desert nomadic societies in which people were so dependent upon one another for continued existence. This regulation also applied to the sojourner in the land (12:19), a resident alien who was required to observe the laws of the land but was not obligated to worship its deity (cf. Exod. 22:21; Num. 15:15, 16; Lev. 25:23). The festival was marked by a holy convocation of the people on the first day and another on the seventh, with no work done on those days.

3. *Observance of the first Passover* (12:21-36)

Moses called the elders of Israel together and repeated the instructions God had given him for killing and eating the passover lamb. They were to dip hyssop in the animal's blood and touch the lintel and doorposts with the hyssop. Hyssop was a small bushy plant usually identified as the herb marjoram, mentioned only eight times in the Old Testament. When the Lord passed through the land to slay the Egyptians, He would pass over the homes protected by the mark of blood. Those who remained inside the marked houses would not be killed.

The Israelites were instructed to continue to observe the Passover for all time after they entered the land God was going to give them. In answer to their children's questions about the meaning of the observance, they were to reply, "It is the sacrifice of the LORD's passover, who passed over the houses of the children of Israel in Egypt, when he smote the Egyptians, and delivered our houses" (12:27). Passover still is characterized in Jewish homes by a question and answer period in which the father retells the familiar story of release from Egyptian slavery.

At midnight the Lord smote all the firstborn in Egypt from Pharaoh's firstborn to the firstborn of the captive in the dungeon (12:29; literally, the "pit house") and all the firstborn of the cattle; there was not a house that escaped death. Such an anguished cry arose in Egypt that Pharaoh himself joined the demand for the Israelites to leave the land at once. The hitherto proud ruler frantically appealed to Moses even as he ordered them to leave the land, "Bless me also" (12:30-32). It was a catastrophic blow not only against the Egyptian people but also against their religion. Pharaoh was considered to be a god; his firstborn son who would succeed him would be a god also; yet they were both powerless to protect the nation or even the royal household from the common fate of all Egypt. The real significance of the tenth and last plague lay in the fact that it represented the defeat of the Egyptian gods (12:12); they were powerless against the God of Moses. It also served as punishment upon the Egyptians, who for more than eighty years had been killing all the male Israelite babies they could apprehend (unless the order in 1:22 was later rescinded).

The Israelites carefully carried out Moses' instructions. They took their unleavened dough and kneading bowls together with the great quantities of gold and silver jewelry the Egyptians had given them. They took their plunder and, like a victorious army loaded with the spoils of battle, set out on their journey to the Promised Land.

B. Israel's Departure From Egypt (12:37-51)

The people journeyed from Rameses to Succoth (usually equated with modern Tell el-Maskhutah near Lake Timsah at the eastern end of the Wadi Tumilat), about thirty miles away. We are told there were about six hundred thousand men, not counting women and children; the figure implies a total of at least two million people, perhaps three million. The number generally is corroborated elsewhere (Exod. 38:26; Num. 1:46; 11:21) which would rule out an error in textual transmission. The sheer logistics of food supplies for so many is staggering, apart from the problems of maintaining order and communication among so many as they traveled. How could such a large group have moved through the sea in one night or all assembled at Sinai? How could Moses have sprinkled blood on two million people (24:8)?

Because so many problems present themselves, various solutions for reducing the numbers to manageable proportions have been proposed. Some suppose that the number was the error of a scribe in copying (6000 instead of 600,000). Others suggest that the number is figurative (as is much language in the Old Testament) and communicates the idea of power and victory through exaggeration (cf. 1 Sam. 18:7). A number of scholars have pointed out that the number "thousand" in "six hundred thousand" is a word that can also mean a military unit, a clan, or the leader of a tribal group (thus, six hundred units, clans, or leaders). A few have argued that the number is from the census of David (2 Sam. 24) that somehow got misplaced. Another group of scholars believes the number is part of an etiological legend written much later without a historical basis, a kind of epic literary composition to explain the origins of the Israelite nation. These scholars arbitrarily reduce the number to a few thousand at most who left Egypt, and justify the reduction by Deuteronomy 7:7, which says the number was small. However, any attempt to reduce the number of participants creates other problems. If only a few thousand people were involved in the Exodus, why were the Egyptians afraid of them and why were they subjected to slavery to reduce their numbers (Exod. 1:9)? Why did the people have such anxiety about food supplies (16:2,3)? Why were the burdens of settling disputes among the people so time-consuming for Moses (18:13-23)? And why were the Moabites terrified of them (Num. 22:3)? The fact that no solution has commended itself to a majority of scholars serves as warning that any attempt to reduce the numbers may solve some problems but at the same time will create others. Whatever the exact number may have been, the miraculous intervention of God was required to effect Israel's release.

As if the problem of numbers were not already sufficient, a mixed multitude (literally, "swarm," the same word used to describe a swarm of flies in 8:21) went out with the Israelites (12:38). These were non-Israelites; perhaps some were Egyptians who had intermarried with Israelite prisoners of war and other enslaved groups. Some may themselves have been Egyptian slaves. Later this group would prove to be a snare to the Israelites (Num. 11:4).

We are told that the total time the Israelites spent in Egypt was 430 years (12:40). However, Genesis 15:13 says "four hundred years" (cf. Acts 7:6), but this difference can be explained as a rounding off of 430. Does the text mean 430 years from the time of Abraham's arrival in Canaan or from Jacob's descent into Egypt (cf. Gal. 3:17)? The Septuagint, apparently in recognizing the problem, says the sojourn in Egypt and in Canaan totaled 430 years, but the period in Egypt alone amounted to 215 years.

In what amounts to a play on the Hebrew word "watch" (*shamar*), we are told that it was a night in which the Lord kept watch over His people, and thereafter they would observe it as a night of watching (12:42). Passover still is observed each year in Jewish homes, and is their most important home festival. It is celebrated for eight days (seven days by Reform Jews) during March or April (the date varies each year as does the Christian date for Easter). The highlight of the celebration is the Seder service, a festive family meal that is observed with a traditional ceremony that includes the retelling of the Exodus story, a menu of hard-boiled eggs dipped in salt water, roasted meat on a bone, bitter herbs, a mixture of nuts and apples, matzah bread, and four glasses of wine. Each part of the meal has its own symbolic meaning. The meal is observed in leisurely fashion, not in haste as was the first Passover, with the father sitting at the head of the table, leaning on a pillow. After the destruction of the Temple in A.D. 70, the custom of sacrificing a lamb was discarded from the observance.

The Passover was to be a distinctively Israelitish celebration; no foreigner, sojourner, or hired servant could participate in it, though circumcised slaves who had been purchased could share in the meal

(12:43-45). The people were told not to break any of the bones of the passover lamb (12:46; cf. Ps. 34:20 and John 19:36). No uncircumcised person could participate in the Passover (12:48), which meant that strangers among the Israelites who wanted to observe the Passover were required to submit to circumcision.

C. Dedication of the Firstborn (13:1-16)

At the same time death was being visited upon the firstborn of the Egyptians, God commanded Moses concerning the Israelites: "Sanctify unto me all the firstborn, whatsoever openeth the womb among the children of Israel, both of man and of beast" (13:2). The firstborn occupied a place of special privilege among ancient Semites. Many of them believed that the firstborn belonged to the deity and had to be sacrificed to him; child sacrifice was widely practiced and was not unknown in early Israel (Gen. 22:2,3; Judg. 11:34-39; 2 Sam. 21:9). In the Old Testament "firstborn" (defined as that which first opens the womb) is most frequently used to designate the eldest son. His privileges and responsibilities included succession to the headship of the family and responsibility for continuation and well being of the family. He received preferential treatment (Gen. 43:33), a double portion of the family inheritance (Deut. 21:17), and the family blessing (Gen. 27:1-4,35-37).

Moses went to the people with the command concerning the firstborn, after reminding them to remember the day that they came out of Egypt and into a land "flowing with milk and honey" by observing the Feast of Unleavened Bread at the appointed time each year (13:5). The feast would be for a sign on their hand and a memorial between their eyes (13:9; cf. Deut. 6:8). Other peoples often had a mark branded or tattooed on the hand or another part of the body with the name or symbol of the deity they worshiped and whose protection they enjoined to ward off evil spirits. Sometimes they wore a sacred badge or jeweled ornament on the forehead as a symbol of devotion to their god. For the Israelites the Passover with its Feast of Unleavened Bread, not tattoos or other external symbols, would serve as their identification with their deity.

Then Moses told them that after entering Canaan they would set apart every firstborn of the males to the Lord for sacrifice (13:11-13). The firstborn of a donkey was to be redeemed by the substitution of a lamb (perhaps because the donkey was considered unclean, and therefore unfit for sacrifice, cf. 34:20; Num. 18:15), or else the owner was required to break the neck of the animal. The firstborn male of animals was to be sacrificed to the Lord, but the firstborn son was to be redeemed (Exod. 13:13; 34:20). This provision is an important reminder that human sacrifice was never sanctioned by God (Deut. 18:10; Lev. 18:21; 20:2-5), though the Israelites themselves gave their children as sacrifice, as did their pagan neighbors (cf. 2 Kings 3:27; 16:3; 17:31; 21:6; 2 Chron. 33:6; Ezek. 16:20,21). The prophets constantly spoke out against this abhorrent practice (cf. Isa. 57:4,5; Jer. 7:30-34; 19:4-9; 44:6-10; Ezek. 16:20).

The price of redemption of the firstborn is not given in Exodus 13:13, but Numbers 18:16 fixed the price at five shekels in silver. The word found in 13:13 for "redeem" (Hebrew, *padah*) always is used of persons and living beings in the Old Testament; it is a term from commercial law and emphasizes payment (the New Testament equivalent is *agorazō*, from a word meaning "to buy at the market place," Gal. 3:13; Rev. 5:9). In its secular usage redemption was the recovery by payment of something for its original owner that had been alienated from him. Sometimes instead of redeeming a son Israelite parents devoted their son to the Lord for service as priests, as in the case of Samuel (1 Sam. 1:11,22).

D. Crossing of the Red Sea (13:17–15:21)

1. *Divine guidance by day and night* (13:17-22)

God did not take the Israelites to Canaan by the shortest route, along the north edge of the Suez isthmus, then along the coast to Gaza, a journey that would have required perhaps two weeks at the most, for that route would have taken them through the land of the Philistines (13:17). The people, so recently set free from their years of bondage, were not physically or psychologically ready to fight an enemy and might have returned to Egypt.

The mention of the Philistines at this juncture in history appears to be an anachronism, as the Philistines actually did not settle on the eastern Mediterranean coast until about 1188 B.C., after their abortive attempt to settle in Egypt was thwarted by Rameses III. After they were driven from his shores, they settled on the eastern Mediterranean coast in the land that later received its name from them, Palestine. It can be explained as the same kind of anachronism as calling the thirteen American colonies the "United States" or referring to the land of the Aztecs by its later, better-known name, Mexico.

There were already strong and powerful cities in the region which the Israelites would have been forced to fight, had they gone directly to Canaan from Egypt. Instead, God led them by way of the wilderness toward the Red Sea (13:18; literally "Sea of Reeds"). The exact identity of this body of water has caused considerable discussion among scholars. It could not be the body of water we know as the Red Sea, which is about 130-250 miles wide. It usually is identified as the marshy district of Lake Timsah north of the Gulf of Suez, at the entrance of Goshen. But as has been observed by several scholars, the knowledge of the exact location of the body of water through which the Israelites passed is no more central to their faith than our knowledge of the exact location of the cross or tomb of Jesus.

Moses remembered to take the bones of Joseph with them in fulfillment of a pledge that Joseph had exacted of the Israelites before his death (Gen. 50:25). Even in his lifetime Joseph knew that Egypt was not the permanent abode of God's people. He remembered the promise of the land of Canaan that had been given to Abraham, renewed with his grandfather Isaac, and his father Jacob, and it was in that land he desired to be buried. He was finally laid to rest at Shechem after the Israelites had entered Canaan and occupied it under Joshua (Josh. 24:32). The first stopping places along the way were Succoth and Etham, the exact locations of which are uncertain; they were somewhere on the edge of the desert country at the eastern frontier of Egypt.

So that the people could travel day and night in order to increase the distance between them and Pharaoh, the Lord went (the Hebrew word could be translated "continually went") with the Israelites in a pillar of cloud by day and in a pillar of fire by night (13:21). The pillar of cloud and fire have been understood by some scholars as smoking and burning braziers that were carried on tall poles in front of the army and could be seen some distance away. Whatever their exact form, these visible symbols of God's presence were constantly in front of the people, leading them onward.

2. Pursuit by Pharaoh (14:1-14)

God instructed Moses to tell the people to turn back and encamp in front of Pi-hahiroth (an Egyptian name that means "region of salt marshes," or perhaps "house of the goddess Hathor"), between Migdol ("tower" or "fortress") and the sea, toward Baal-zephon ("lord of the north"). Pharaoh would be tempted to pursue them, seeing that they were shut in with the sea in front, hopelessly entangled (literally, "perplexed," "confused," "wandering aimlessly") in the wilderness. When Pharaoh saw that the Israelites were unable to go forward, he would forget his agreement to free them and would pursue them to bring them back to Egypt. In the ensuing victory over Pharaoh and his army, God would receive honor, and the Egyptians would know that He was the Lord (14:4).

Even as God had said, when Pharaoh heard that the Israelites had left Egypt, he assembled his army and six hundred picked chariots for pursuit. When the Israelites saw the dust of the approaching army, they were terrified and turned on Moses and accused him of bringing them into the wilderness to die. They reminded him that they had told him in Egypt to leave them alone. Slavery in Egypt was preferable to death in the wilderness! This is the first recorded complaint of the Israelites, but not the last which Moses and God would hear in the years ahead.

There are two traditions reflected in the Old Testament of the attitude of the Israelites during the wilderness years; one is that of a rebellious people (Exod. 15:24; 16:2; 17:3; etc.; Ezek. 20:13); the other is that of a faithful people (Hos. 2:14,15; Jer. 2:2).[1] Some scholars have tried to set the two traditions against each other as contradictory. They say the murmuring tradition developed among the priestly group in Jerusalem as a polemic against the northern kingdom of Israel that was arguing God could be worshiped in Dan and Bethel. It was as if the people of Judah were saying, "You Israelites have always been a faithless people." However, a better solution is to accept both traditions as correct — some of the people trusted the Lord; others did not; there were times when they followed by faith; there were other times when they rebelled against God. The Israelites had not learned a New Testament lesson they sorely needed — the best remedy for a complaining spirit is to give thanks in everything (1 Thess. 5:18).

Moses did not rebuke the people for their murmurings, but said to them, "Fear ye not, stand still, and see the salvation of the Lord, which he will shew to you to-day" (14:13). Salvation is used here in its original sense, "to be spacious, broad"; hence the idea of freedom or deliverance is inherent in the word. Only later did it assume the theological overtones associated with it today. The further command, "hold your peace" (14:14; "be still," rsv, from a word that means to be silent, dumb, speechless), would surely test the faith of an activist-oriented person

---

[1]See George W. Coats, *Rebellion in the Wilderness* (Nashville: Abingdon Press, 1968), for a full discussion of the murmuring motif in the wilderness.

who is not quite sure whether God can accomplish anything without man's help. Israel was about to learn that God provides a way of escape when there seems to be none (cf. 1 Cor. 10:13).

3. Crossing through the parted waters (14:15-22)

As if their faith were not being tried severely enough by the command to do nothing to defend themselves, God also told Moses to tell the people to go forward toward the sea that lay before them. He told Moses to lift his rod and point it toward the sea and the waters would separate so the Israelites could cross over on dry ground. In addition, God would harden the hearts of the Egyptians so they would pursue the Israelites, thus providing the opportunity for God to have a great victory over them.

Then the angel of God (14:19; literally, "messenger of God," a term not found frequently, the equivalent of the "angel of the Lord") who had gone in front of the Israelites (cf. John 10:4) now went behind them. The pillar of cloud also moved behind them to separate the Israelites from the Egyptians throughout the night. Then Moses lifted up his rod toward the sea, and the Lord sent a strong east wind all night that separated the waters, and the people of Israel were able to pass through on dry ground with a wall of water on either side. Many explanations have been advanced to account for the miracle of the crossing at the Sea of Reeds, but whatever the explanation proposed, clearly the Israelites interpreted it as a miraculous intervention of God on their behalf.[2]

4. Destruction of the Egyptian army (14:23-31)

When the Egyptians saw the Israelites escaping through the dry passageway in the midst of the waters, they pursued them into the riverbed without hesitation. The Lord slowed their pursuit by causing the heavy chariot wheels to bog down in the wet sand (14:25; "took off their chariot wheels," KJV; the Hebrew word literally means "turn aside"). The exact nature of the problem the Egyptians were encountering with their chariots is uncertain, but in some way they were slowed down. In panic they called to one another to flee, for they saw that God was fighting on the side of the Israelites (14:25). However, before they

---

[2]Even a liberal scholar like Martin Noth concedes that it is better not to seek "natural" explanations here: ". . . is clearly speaking here of a divine miracle; and it is extremely questionable whether it is appropriate to look for a 'natural' parallel for the events he describes and thus seek to explain the whole 'naturally.'" Martin Noth, *Exodus* (Philadelphia: The Westminster Press, 1962), p. 116.

could escape, God told Moses to stretch out his hand to bring the waters back upon the Egyptians, their chariots, and their horsemen. When Moses did so, the waters rushed together and covered all the army of Pharaoh that had followed the Israelites into the sea; not one of them escaped. There is no necessity to insist Pharaoh died with his army. Egyptian records do not mention such a death nor does the biblical account require this interpretation.

The Israelites stood on the other shore and watched the destruction of the Egyptian army. What they saw caused them to fear the Lord and to believe in Him and in His servant Moses (14:31; the Hebrew word for "believe" is the same root as the word used to end prayers, "Amen," and comes from a word meaning "to confirm," "to support"). "Servant" is used to describe Moses elsewhere in the Pentateuch only in Numbers 12:7,8 and Deuteronomy 34:5; it is frequently used of him in Joshua. Though the Israelites saw and believed, the New Testament reminds us that greater is the faith of those who "have not seen and yet have believed" (John 20:29, NIV).

5. Songs in praise of deliverance (15:1-21)

Chapter 14 is a narrative account of the deliverance of Israel from the Egyptians at the Sea of Reeds. Chapter 15 describes the same event in poetry in the form of victory songs, one sung by Moses (15:1-18; variously called the Song of Moses, the Song of the Sea, the Victory Hymn of Moses, Moses' Song of Triumph, the Song of the Reed Sea, a Hymn of Praise) and the other by his sister Miriam (15:19-21, called the Song of Miriam). The theme of both is praise of God for the glorious victory over Israel's enemy. The songs have been lauded as being among the finest examples of Hebrew poetry, notable for their vivid imagery, their poetic fire, and exuberant spirit of triumph. They are generally dated very early, even by scholars who would not grant an early date for most of the rest of the Pentateuch. Some, however, have argued for a date after the conquest for the first song, as verses 13-17 seem to suggest that the wilderness wanderings and conquest of Canaan are already events of the past.

The first verse states the theme of the first song: praise to the Lord for the glorious defeat of the Egyptians. Verses 2 and 3 continue the theme of praise by acknowledging that the Lord is the source of strength and deliverance (the short form Yah, "Lord," instead of the usual Yahweh, is found in verse 2; it also appears in the word "hallelujah," which means "Praise the Lord"). The Lord is described as a "man of war" (15:3). The theme of God as warrior, the One who fights the battles of His people, recurs frequently in the Old Testament (e.g., Deut. 1:30; Josh. 5:13-15; 2 Chr. 20:29).

Exodus 15:4-12 give the details of Israel's deliverance from Pharaoh's army. The enemy is pictured as sinking into the waters of the sea like a stone, shattered by the right hand of the Lord. The separation of the waters that permitted the Israelites to pass through on dry land is attributed to the blast of the nostrils of God (15:8; an anthropomorphic way of referring to the east wind that God had sent to separate the waters; cf. 14:21). The enemy is represented as being determined to pursue the Israelites and destroy them by the sword, only to sink (literally, "went gurgling down") like lead in the waters that sweep over them, impelled by a mighty wind sent by God (15:10). The song affirms the uniqueness of God: "Who is like unto thee, O LORD, among the gods?" (15:11). Some have interpreted this verse to be an acknowledgment of the existence of other gods but the selection of only one of them to worship (called monolatry). However, it could just as well be understood as a denial of the reality of other gods.

The song closes (15:13-18) by comparing God's guidance of His people to the unchangeable love (KJV, "mercy"; RSV, "steadfast love"; a word that most frequently is used in the Old Testament to describe God's unfailing covenant love) of the shepherd who guides his sheep to a watering place. The Philistines (see comment on 13:17 for possible anachronism), Edomites, Moabites, and Canaanites hear of the fate of the Egyptians and are terrified. They are helpless ("still as a stone," 15:16) to hinder the advance of the Israelites, God's purchased people. God has redeemed Israel from bondage, as a slave is purchased, to be His own possession. He will bring the people into the land He has chosen for His abode, the sanctuary which His hands have established. Some have taken the reference to the sanctuary in verse 17 to mean the sanctuary at Shiloh or the temple in Jerusalem, but it should be understood as the entire Promised Land. It is a sanctuary (literally, "a separated place," that is, holy) because it is the place where God will dwell.

Verses 19-21 contain the Song of Miriam, called a prophetess in verse 20. Other prophetesses mentioned in the Old Testament are Deborah (Judg. 4:4), Huldah (2 Kings 22:14), Nodiah (Neh. 6:14, a false prophetess), and Isaiah's wife (Isa. 8:3). An evaluation of the position of women in Old Testament times that denigrates them overlooks the leadership roles they exercised from time to time (prophetesses like Miriam, military leaders like Deborah, autocratic rulers like Athaliah). A prose summary is given in verses 19,20, and the brief song she sang is preserved in verse 21 (cf. 15:1, where the wording is almost identical). The brevity of the song is taken by scholars as evidence of its authenticity and antiquity. Miriam is described as celebrating the victory over the Egyptians by leading the other women in a display of ecstatic dancing, accompanied by the timbrel (an instrument like the tambourine). The emotional fervor and spirit of exultation communicated in both songs of chapter 15 can only be explained as spontaneous utterances by eyewitnesses to the great drama at the Sea of Reeds. Such a spirit of triumph and praise could not have been captured by a poet writing centuries after the event.

For Further Study

1. In a Bible dictionary or encyclopedia (see bibliography) read articles on: Passover, Feast of Unleavened Bread, Firstborn, Red Sea (Sea of Reeds).

2. Make a comparative study of the way the first Passover was celebrated and the way it is observed in Judaism today. What are the similarities and what are the differences?

3. Does the emphasis on the firstborn in the Old Testament seem to relegate other children in the family to roles of lesser importance in God's sight? Can you think of some important biblical people who were not the firstborn?

4. How can you harmonize the exultation over the defeat of the Egyptians with the New Testament injunction, "Love your enemies"?

5. What valid comparisons can you make between Israel's exodus from Egypt and the Christian's experience of deliverance from sin through redemption in Christ?

Chapter 6

Journey to Sinai

(Exodus 15:22–18:27)

With the memory of victory over the Egyptians fresh in their minds, the Israelites should have journeyed from the Sea of Reeds to Mount Sinai with complete confidence in God's ability to take care of them. But instead, the journey was marked by complaints (15:24; 16:2), disobedience to God's instructions (16:27,28), faultfinding (17:2), and disputes with one another (18:16). However, God was faithful to His promises. He had told Moses that He would bring the people to Sinai (3:12), and He did. This chapter is the account of that journey.

A. The First Stops Along the Way (15:22-27)

1. *Water provided at Marah* (15:22-26)

From the Sea of Reeds Moses led his people into the wilderness of Shur, located somewhere on the northeast border of Egypt. "Shur" is a word usually taken to mean "wall," but its etymology is uncertain; it is equated with Etham in Numbers 33:8. They traveled for three days in the wilderness without finding water, a distance of perhaps thirty to forty miles, for a nomad with flocks and herds could travel about ten to fifteen miles a day. When they came to the spring Marah, they found water, but it was so bitter they could not drink it. Marah is from a word that means "bitter"; its exact location is uncertain though it has been identified with modern 'Ain Hawarah or Ayun Musa. With their complaint, "What shall we drink?" ringing in his ears, Moses cried to the Lord for help. God instructed him to cast a nearby tree with purifying qualities into the water, whereupon the water became palatable (15:25; literally, "sweet"). The Lord then told the people that if they would diligently obey Him, He would bring none of the diseases on them He had inflicted on the Egyptians, for He was their "healer." God as healer here refers to making the water sweet (cf. 2 Kings 2:21,22; Ezek. 47:8, where the same word is used for the "healing" of water), but the word is used more frequently in the Old Testament for physical and spiritual healing (Gen. 20:17; 1 Sam. 6:3; 2 Chron. 7:14; 30:20; Pss. 103:3; 147:3; Isa. 53:5; Jer. 3:22; 6:14; 30:17; Hos. 6:1, where it means forgiveness).

2. Encampment at Elim (15:27)

The Israelites next encamped at Elim, a desert oasis with twelve springs of water and seventy palm trees (cf. Num. 33:9). The word "Elim" is from a word meaning "a great tree," perhaps the terebinth tree. Earlier the word was thought to mean "gods" and, if so, Elim may have been a sacred site for nomads living in that area. It has been identified as Wadi Gharandel, which is some sixty miles from Suez on the west side of the Sinai peninsula. Elim, however, as pleasant as it may have appeared to the weary Israelites, was not the Promised Land, and they had to move on.

B. Manna and Quails Provided in the Wilderness of Sin (16:1-36)

1. Hunger of the people satisfied (16:1-21)

After leaving Elim, the Israelites came to the wilderness of Sin (mentioned elsewhere only twice, in 17:1 and Num. 33:11,12). The name "Sin" here should not be mistaken for one of the many Hebrew words for sin found in the Old Testament;[1] rather, it comes from a word that means thorny, or perhaps clay. It is related linguistically to the word for "Sinai" and to the bush (seneh) of 3:2; its use here is intended to describe the nature of the terrain.

The Israelites had been traveling for a month since leaving Egypt (16:1; cf. 12:6,31), and having exhausted all their food supplies they began to complain to Moses: "Would to God we had died by the hand of the Lord in the land of Egypt, when we sat by the flesh pots, and when we did eat bread to the full" (16:3). They had lost confidence in God's ability to lead them and to provide for them, and like Lot's wife (Gen. 19:26), took a backward look to life in Egypt that now seemed preferable. Their memories were obviously faulty, for as slaves they could not have had enough to eat. The "flesh pots" they longed for were kettles full

---

[1]It is true that the journey from Egypt to the Promised Land has frequently been compared to the Christian life — release from the bondage of sin, baptism through water, a time of trial and testing, provision by God for all needs, and arrival at the final destination. However, the etymology of "Sin" here would not permit a legitimate comparison to an all-too-frequent Christian experience of wandering in sin.

of flesh, but meat was not part of the everyday diet of the poor man or of slaves in Egypt. How like the person who constantly recalls the "good old days," that probably never were quite as good as he remembers them! They accused Moses of bringing them into the wilderness to experience a painful, lingering death by starvation (16:3).

God's response to their complaints and accusations was to tell Moses that He would "rain bread from heaven" for them (bread in the Old Testament frequently means food in general). The ostensible purpose of the heavenly food was to satisfy their hunger, but God said the real purpose was to test the people to see if they would obey Him (16:4; see also Deut. 8:3; cf. the first man and woman's temptation, which was a test of their willingness to obey God, Gen. 2,3). It was the people, not God, who were on trial. They were instructed to gather only enough of the heaven-sent food each day for that day; on the sixth day they would gather twice as much so there would be food for the Sabbath.

Moses told the people that through the provision of food they would see the glory of the Lord (see 33:18ff. for discussion of the glory of the Lord). Then Moses angrily reminded them that their murmurings were not against him and Aaron but were against the Lord (16:8). Moses instructed Aaron to call the people together; they looked toward the wilderness where they saw the glory of the Lord in the cloud (16:10). God then told Moses He had heard the murmurings of the people and promised that they would eat flesh that very evening and the next morning they would be filled with bread. Then they would know that He was the Lord their God. Two distinct foods are mentioned here, bread (manna) and flesh (quail), although the focus of attention is given to the manna.

In the evening quail came up and alighted in the camp, covering the ground. These migratory birds can still be observed on the Sinai peninsula traveling in vast numbers. When they alight, they are exhausted and can easily be captured by hand in great quantities (cf. Num. 11:31-34, where the provision of quail is an expression of the Lord's anger with his people rather than an act of gracious provision).

The next morning a dew covered the ground. When it evaporated, a small substance like hoarfrost remained on the ground. When the people saw it, they questioned one another. "What is it?" (16:15; Hebrew, literally *man hu*, hence the name "manna" that was given to it). It looked like coriander seed, was white, and tasted like wafers made with honey (16:31). Moses told them that it was to serve as the bread the Lord had promised them. He instructed them carefully concerning the time for gathering and the amount to be collected. They were to gather one omer (about two quarts) for each person to a tent and were not to keep any of it overnight (cf. Paul's application in 2 Cor. 8:14,15). Some of the people did not listen to Moses and kept some of the manna till the next day, only to discover that it bred worms and became foul smelling. The manna that was not gathered each morning melted when the sun became hot.

Many scholars have pointed out that several desert plants, notably the tamarisk tree, exude a sweet sticky substance that drips to the ground, turning white as it crystallizes, and tastes like honey. Others believe that it is the excretion of certain insects. This substance is still called *mann* by Arabs living in the region, who use it like honey after boiling and straining it. These scholars believe this was the "food" the Israelites found in the wilderness. These explanations, however, leave unanswered questions. There are some features of the biblical manna that do not fit the modern *mann.* How could such excretions (whether from a tree or from insects) provide enough food each day for even a few hundred people, let alone thousands? How would this explain the tradition among the Israelites that this food was available to them throughout the rest of their journey to Canaan and only ceased after they entered the land (Josh. 5:12)? How can it be compared to modern *mann,* that does not breed worms or melt, is not white in color, and is not made into cakes? Why did it appear only on six days (16:25,26)? To shrug off such questions as unimportant is not really being intellectually honest. Biblical manna does have similarities to a substance that can be collected in the desert today, but it remains a unique phenomenon.

2. *Regulations for manna on the Sabbath* (16:22-30)

On the sixth day the people gathered twice as much manna, two omers apiece. Moses reminded the leaders of the congregation that the next day was the Sabbath, a day of rest (from a word "to cease," "to rest"). The people were to bake and boil the manna as they desired, keeping the remainder for the next day. The people did as Moses commanded, and the next day they discovered that the manna they had kept did not become foul-smelling or breed worms. Some of the people, however, went out on the seventh day to gather manna but found none. The Lord rebuked them for their disobedience and told them that they were not to go out to do any work on the seventh day. This is the earliest passage in the Old Testament that mentions the Sabbath day. It reminds us that the Sabbath was already observed in Israel before it was incorporated into the Ten Commandments given at Sinai (see discussion at 20:8-11, for a history of the Sabbath; cf. Deut. 5:12-15).

3. *Manna kept as a memorial* (16:31-36)

Moses instructed the people to fill a jar with an omer of manna and place it before the Lord in front of the Testimony to be kept perpetually. The "Testimony" was either the ark of the covenant, a chest which contained the Decalogue, or it was another way of referring to the Decalogue itself. As the tabernacle had not yet been constructed, the instruction given at this time could not be carried out until later. Hebrews 9:4 preserves a tradition that the manna was kept in a golden pot along with Aaron's rod that budded (cf. Num. 17:10) and the tables of the law, which were kept in (not in front of) the ark. In an obvious comparison to the manna of the Old Testament, John 6:58 calls Jesus the bread from heaven.

C. Other Evidences of the Divine Presence (17:1-16)

1. *Water from a rock at Rephidim* (17:1-7)

The Israelites moved on from the wilderness of Sin and camped at Rephidim (location unknown, perhaps the Wadi Refayid) according to the commandment of the Lord (17:1; literally, "according to the mouth of the Lord"). Another crisis arose when the people discovered there was no water to drink. They contended with Moses, blaming him for their predicament, and demanded that he give them water to drink. Moses responded by asking why they contended with him. He made it clear that their argument was with God: "Why do you test the Lord?" (17:2). The KJV says, "Wherefore do ye tempt the Lord?" but this is a misleading translation. "Tempt" usually suggests the idea of enticing to do wrong, but the Hebrew word here, *nissah*, means to test or to prove; it is the same word used concerning Abraham (Gen. 22:1). God tests a person by subjecting him to a trial to determine whether his loyalty is sincere or to strengthen that loyalty. More frequently, however, man tests God because of unbelief.

Israel still was not convinced that God was in their midst and was able to supply all their needs. The people were thirsty, and they accused Moses of bringing them out of Egypt to kill them, their children, and their cattle with thirst (17:3). In a moment of despair, perhaps tinged with self-pity, Moses cried to the Lord, "What shall I do unto this people? they be almost ready to stone me" (17:4). Without a hint of displeasure at the people's complaining attitude, God instructed Moses to take some of the elders, and with the rod he had used to strike the Nile (7:20), to strike a rock at Horeb and water would come out for the people to drink. Horeb is another name for Sinai (cf. 3:1), but here it must refer to a larger geographical area with Sinai as a particular peak, as Horeb (or Sinai) itself was not reached till later (19:1). Moses struck the rock in the presence of the elders, as God had instructed him, and the water gushed out to satisfy the thirsty Israelites (cf. Num. 20:7-12, where Moses struck a rock to provide water for the people and incurred the wrath of God; and 1 Cor. 10:4 for Paul's christological interpretation of the same event). Rational explanations of the miraculous supply of water cite parallels where water has poured out of certain desert rock formations when the surface of the rock is broken. Moses called the place Massah ("testing," from *nissah;* see discussion at 17:2) and Meribah (from a word *rib,* "to strive," "to argue"), because it was the place where they tested the Lord and argued with Moses (17:2) by asking, "Is the LORD among us, or not?" (17:7). It was unusual but not impossible for a place to have two names.

2. *Victory over the Amalekites* (17:8-16)

Food and water shortages were not the only problems the Israelites encountered in their journey to Canaan. At Rephidim they were forced to fight against the nomadic Amalekites (descendants of Esau according to Gen. 36:12). Moses instructed Joshua (17:9; here is mentioned for the first time) to choose men to fight against the Amalekites. Moses, together with Aaron and Hur (mentioned elsewhere only in 24:14, and husband of Miriam according to an ancient tradition) went to the top of a hill to watch the progress of the battle. As long as Moses held his hand up (variously interpreted as a gesture of prayer, encouragement for Israel, a blessing on Israel or a curse on the enemy, a signal to advance, or a symbol of magical potency) Israel prevailed, but when he became tired and lowered his hand, the Amalekites prevailed.

Finally, Aaron and Hur found a stone for the aged leader to sit upon, and they held up his hands, one man on either side until sunset, thereby enabling Joshua to discomfit (17:13; "mow down," RSV; but literally, "weaken") the enemy. The verb suggests that the victory was less than total; the Israelites had not heard the last of the Amalekites.

The Lord told Moses to write as a memorial in a book that He would blot out the Amalekites completely. This is one of the rare references made to Moses recording the events of the journey to Canaan and is ignored by critics who do not acknowledge Mosaic authorship for any part of the Pentateuch.

To commemorate the victory, Moses built an altar and called it Jehovah-nissi (17:15; "The Lord is my banner") because of the Lord's solemn vow to continue His warfare against the Amalekites from generation to generation. "Banner" is from a word that means "be high," "be conspicuous." Armies customarily carried an insignia or banner into battle at the head of their troops to serve as a rallying point. Moses seemed to be saying that the Lord Himself would be the only banner the Israelites would carry into battle and that they would rally around Him to lead them on to victory.

D. Moses' Reunion With Jethro (18:1-27)

1. A joyful reunion (18:1-9)

News of how the Lord had brought Israel out of Egypt and of all the things He had done for Moses and the people reached Jethro, the priest of Midian (never called "priest of Yahweh") and Moses' father-in-law. We are told here that Jethro had taken back Zipporah, Moses wife, after Moses sent her away (18:2). No other reference is made to this event, and one can only surmise what actually happened. Zipporah was last mentioned in 4:24-26, when she was on her way to Egypt with her husband, so she must have been sent back sometime after that. Some have supposed that Moses was angered by the harshness of his wife's words upon the occasion of the circumcision of their son (4:25,26) and sent her away then (in later times this term, "to send away," would mean divorce, but not here). Perhaps he realized that he would be in Egypt only a short time and it would be impractical and unnecessary for his wife and family to go with him so he sent them back to stay with her father. Zipporah was sent back with their two sons, Gershom and Eliezer (18:3,4)

Jethro, together with Zipporah and the two sons, went out to the wilderness to meet Moses where he was encamped at the mountain of God. When Moses was informed of their approach, he went out to meet them and received his father-in-law with the usual effusive Oriental deference, bowing himself down before the priest and kissing him. They asked each other of their welfare (18:7; literally "peace") and went into a tent where Moses told his father-in-law all that had happened in Egypt and how the Lord had delivered them. It seems strange that no mention is made of Moses' reunion with his wife and children, but the omission need not be interpreted as proof of alienation between the couple or a slight on Moses' part, intentional or unintentional. Interpretations based on silence of the Scriptures can sometimes be misleading; such omissions are characteristic of the Hebrew literary style that frequently fails to record events not deemed central to the story being narrated. When Jethro heard all the good things God had done for Israel by delivering them from the Egyptians, he rejoiced (18:9; a rare word in the Old Testament; elsewhere found only in Job 3:6 and Ps. 21:6; it can also mean "to sharpen").

2. Sacrifices offered to God by Jethro (18:10-12)

In an unusual expression of praise, Jethro, upon hearing of God's mighty acts on behalf of Israel, said, "Blessed be the LORD, who hath delivered you out of the hand of the Egyptians . . . Now I know that the LORD is greater than all gods" (18:10,11; cf. 2 Kings 5:15; Dan. 3:29). Then he offered a burnt offering and sacrifices to God. Afterward, Aaron and all the elders of Israel came to join Jethro in a sacrificial meal before God. This kind of meal was frequently shared by representatives of both parties to a covenant.

Jethro's obvious enthusiasm for Israel's deliverance from Egypt and the sacrifice he offered to God raise the question whether Jethro himself was a worshiper of God rather than an idolatrous priest of the Midianites, worshipers of another deity. Though it was not unheard of for a non-Israelite to bless God, whether he knew Him or not (Dan. 3:28), it was unusual. Jethro's words in 18:10,11 have been interpreted by some as normal expressions of a polytheist and by others as the words of a true monotheist. Some have called this the time of Jethro's conversion to Yahweh worship, or if not conversion, a deeper commitment of one who already believed in God. The possibility of Jethro's being a true Yahweh worshiper has been explored by many scholars. Called the Kenite hypothesis because of Jethro's link to the Kenites, the theory holds that Jethro did indeed know Yahweh and was responsible for introducing Moses to Yahweh worship (see chapter 1 for further discussion of the Kenite hypothesis).

3. The appointment of judges to share the burdens (18:13-27)

The next day Moses sat to judge the people, settling their disputes by appeal to the statutes of God and His laws. They inquired of God through Moses, that is, they sought specific answers through a divine oracle from the mouth of Moses. They stood about Moses from morning to evening as he dealt with their cases one by one.

When Jethro saw what was taking place, he sought an explanation from Moses, and when he was told, he remonstrated that what Moses was doing was not good. He told Moses he would wear himself out (18:18; a word that usually means to wither and fade away as a leaf, Ps. 1:3; Jer. 8:13); the task was too much for one person. Jethro counseled Moses to share his responsibilities with others. He proposed that Moses should represent the people before God and teach them the statutes and laws so that they would know how to please God. He advised Moses to select able men (literally, "men of strength"), men who feared God (that is, worshiped God), who were truthful and hated bribes ("covetousness," KJV, but the word means "gain by violence"). (What better qualifications could be found even for today's political leaders?) These men would be put over the people, some in charge of thousands, some over hundreds, some over fifties, and some responsible for as few as ten people (KJV calls them "rulers," but "overseers" would be a better translation). The division of authority would be comparable to a military organization (cf. 1 Sam. 29:2; 2 Sam. 18:1). These men would judge the lesser matters; only the most important and difficult cases would be brought to Moses for settlement.

Jethro concluded his appeal by telling Moses that if he followed Jethro's plan, and if God so commanded him, Moses would be able to endure and the people would be better satisfied. Some have objected that Moses would not take the advice of a foreign priest when in the past he had always depended on God for direct divine communication. They say it was not until later (Num. 11:16-25) that God instructed Moses to share his responsibilities. However, the passage under consideration reveals no tension nor does it suggest that Moses erred or disobeyed God. Jethro told Moses to inaugurate the plan only if God commanded him to do so (18:23). Moses took the advice of (18:24; "hearkened to," KJV; literally, "obeyed") his father-in-law and appointed men to judge the people's disputes. Then he let his father-in-law depart to return to his own country.

Some lessons that can be learned from Moses' attempt to settle all the people's disputes by himself are: (1) the danger of one person trying to do too much; (2) the reminder that the Lord's work is not just the work of one person, but of many; (3) a person can attempt to do so much that he does not do anything well; and (4) organized activity within the church is not necessarily unspiritual, as some have claimed.

For Further Study

1. In a Bible dictionary or encyclopedia (see bibliography) read articles on: Marah, Elim, wilderness of Sin, manna, Rephidim, Massah, Meribah, Amalekites.

2. What lessons can be learned from the murmurings of the Israelites?

3. Review the stipulations concerning the manna and then decide what lessons can be learned from God's provision of manna for the Israelites.

4. Make a careful study of 17:1-7 and Numbers 20:7-11, observing the similarities and differences in the two stories. Why was it a sin on the one occasion to strike the rock to obtain water and not a sin on the other?

5. What do you believe was Jethro's relationship to the God of Moses? Justify your answer.

PART THREE: A NEW RELATIONSHIP

Chapter 7

The Covenant at Sinai. I: Moral Law

(Exodus 19:1–20:21)

Chapters 19-24 of Exodus (along with Genesis 3) have frequently been called the most important chapters of the Old Testament. In these chapters is found the account of the covenant that God made with Israel at Mount Sinai. [1] The covenant was conditioned upon Israel's obedience to laws which were given to the people at Sinai. The rest of the Old Testament contains the story of how Israel responded to the demands of this covenant relationship. Unfortunately, it is largely a story of disobedience, unheeded warnings of the prophets, and punishment. The history of Israel in Old Testament times has been called a "history of failure" — failure to be the people that God wanted them to be.

A. The Appearance of God on Mount Sinai (19:1–20:17)

1. *Invitation to a covenant relationship* (19:1-8)

In the third month (19:1; often translated "new moon"; understood as the first day of the month because it is followed by the specific statement, "on that day") after leaving Egypt, the Israelites finally arrived at Sinai, in fulfillment of the sign God had given Moses (3:12). They pitched their tents at the base of the mountain.

Scholars have long debated the location of Sinai, but no archaeolog-

---

[1] The etymology of the Hebrew word for covenant *(berith)* is uncertain. It may be from a word *barah* ("to eat"; hence, a covenant was made by eating a meal together), or *birtu* ("to fetter," "to bind"; hence, a covenant was a binding of two or more parties), or *berit* ("between"; hence, a covenant was an agreement between parties). Covenant may be defined as a mutual agreement between two or more parties. It frequently appears with the verb "to cut" (to cut a covenant = to make a covenant), perhaps a carryover from the custom of sealing a covenant by walking between the cut up pieces of an animal (Gen. 15:17). Some examples of covenants in the Old Testament are the covenants of Noah (Gen. 9:8-17), Jacob and Laban (Gen. 29:15-20), David and Jonathan (1 Sam. 18:1-4); and David (2 Sam. 7:4-17).

ical evidence (such as Moses' initials carved on a rock!) has been uncovered that would settle the issue, or likely will be. Suggested locations have been northwest Arabia in the vicinity of the Gulf of Aqaba or the northern Sinai peninsula in the vicinity of Kadesh, but for hundreds of years a mountain peak some 7647 feet high in the southern Sinai peninsula called Jebel Musa ("mountain of Moses") has found the greatest number of supporters.

God called Moses to come up on the mountain where He told him of His willingness to enter into a covenant with Israel. It was a covenant based on God's act of deliverance ("I bare you on eagles' wings, and brought you unto myself," 19:4; cf. Deut. 32:11,12) and conditioned on Israel's obedience ("if ye will obey my voice," 19:5). Three blessings were promised the people if they would accept the covenant: (1) "ye shall be a peculiar treasure unto me" (19:5; better translated, "you shall be my own possession," RSV, because the modern usage of "peculiar" suggests a different meaning from the Hebrew, *segullah*, which means "personal possession," "private treasure," "valued property"; cf. 1 Chron. 29:3; Eccl. 2:8, where it is translated "treasure" in the RSV); (2) "ye shall be unto me a kingdom of priests" (19:6; a phrase not found elsewhere in the Old Testament, but see Isa. 61:6 for a similar idea; a kingdom whose people live wholly to serve God, to be mediators for Him, each one enjoying the right of individual access to Him; notice that the concept of the "priesthood of believers" begins here and not in the New Testament, cf. 1 Peter 2:5,9; Rev. 1:6); and (3) "ye shall be unto me . . . an holy nation" (19:6; separated or set apart unto God from all other nations to live lives that will reflect the nature of God; cf. 1 Peter 2:9). Moses repeated the covenant offer to the elders and the people, and they all agreed to accept it: "All that the LORD hath spoken we will do" (19:8).

Why did God choose from among all the nations of the earth the people we know as Jews to enter into a privileged covenant relationship? They were not a great or powerful nation or a repository of the greatest cultural achievements of their times. If one were selecting a promising candidate to be the chosen people, wouldn't mighty Egypt have been a better choice? Deuteronomy 7:7,8 makes clear that the election of Israel was not due to the merit of the people but to the grace of God: "The LORD did not set his love upon you, nor choose you, because ye were more in number than any people; for ye were the fewest of all people: But because the LORD loved you. . . ." In response to a frequently heard comment, "How odd of God to choose the Jews," a Christian could add, "And how odd of God to have chosen me!"

2. Preparations for the appearance of God (19:9-15)

When Moses told God of the people's willingness to make a covenant with Him, He instructed Moses to tell them to prepare for His appearance in a thick cloud so that they would believe forever when they heard God speaking with Moses. They were told to spend two days consecrating themselves (19:10; from the word *qadhash*, meaning "to be separate"; cf. Gen. 35:2; Josh. 3:5), which involved separating themselves from anything that would make them unclean, so that they would be ready for His descent on Mount Sinai on the third day. He gave a solemn warning that no one should ascend the mountain or even touch its base, upon pain of death, whether man or animal. Sexual abstinence was also required as part of the purification rite (19:15; cf. 1 Sam. 21:4,5; 2 Sam. 11:6-11; 1 Cor. 7:5).

3. The appearance of God on Sinai (19:16-25)

On the morning of the third day the people were terrified by the sound of thunder (*qol*, the same word as "voice"; cf. Gen. 22:18; 26:5; Exod. 5:2; 1 Sam. 7:10; Ps. 46:6; Job 37:4, etc.), the blast of a trumpet (*shophar*, literally, "a ram's horn"; it is not certain whether an actual trumpet or some kind of phenomenon associated with the storm is intended), and by the sight of lightning and a thick cloud that settled on the mountain. Moses led the people to the base of the mountain to witness the descent of God to the top of Sinai in the midst of heavy smoke and fire that frequently has been compared to the spectacle of an active volcano. The Lord spoke to Moses and invited him to ascend to the top of the mountain. He told him to warn both people and priests again not to try to break through to gaze at the Lord, lest they perish (19:21,24; cf. Heb. 12:18-24). He also told Moses to go back and bring Aaron with him. If Aaron did actually return with Moses, this fact is nowhere mentioned in the narrative (cf. 20:21).

4. The Ten Commandments (20:1-17)

By way of introducing the law code found in the following chapters of Exodus, it should be noted that the Israelites were not the first, and certainly not the only, people to have written law codes. Other ancient law codes included those of Ur Nammu (Sumerian, ca. 2050 B.C.),

Lipit-Ishtar (Sumerian, ca. 1900 B.C.), Eshnunna (Akkadian, ca. 1875 B.C.), and Hammurabi (Babylonian, ca. 1690 B.C.). No written law codes have been found in ancient Egypt, however, but this anomaly is explained by the status of the pharaoh; he was considered a god and therefore his spoken word at any given moment was law. The purpose of law in ancient times (as well as modern) was to regulate and control interpersonal relationships and also to maintain the stability of community life. For Israel the law had the effect of binding a heretofore heterogeneous group of slaves into a nation that has endured to the present time.

Though the Hebrew law code contained hundreds of laws (the ancient rabbis counted 613 laws in the Pentateuch), its best known section is the Ten Commandments (sometimes called the Decalogue or the Ten Words), which were the first of the laws given to Moses when he returned to the top of Sinai (20:1-17; cf. Deut. 5:6-21, where the wording of several of the commandments is slightly different). At the outset some general observations should be made concerning the Commandments. They are presented as a revelation from God and therefore should be taken seriously. Because they deal with the most basic moral principles that govern human relationships, they are universal in scope and applicable to all peoples of all ages and of whatever cultural background. No individual or society is better off by ignoring them.

The form in which the Commandments are stated merits attention before examining the individual verses.[2] They are apodictic in form (that is, stated in terms of absolutes, "Thou shalt . . . Thou shalt not . . ."), an expression of law rarely found outside of Israel in the ancient world. A more common mode of expressing law was casuistic (that is, conditional, "If you do thus and so, then I will do thus and so").

A second characteristic of the form of the commandments is the negative way in which they are stated; eight of the ten are expressed negatively ("Thou shalt not . . ."). This negative statement of God's

[2]Many Old Testament scholars have tried to establish parallels between the form of the Sinai covenant and ancient Hittite covenants (cf. Dewey M. Beegle, *Moses, The Servant of Yahweh* (Grand Rapids: William B. Eerdmans Publishing Company, 1972); W. Beyerlin, *Origin and History of the Oldest Sinaitic Tradition* (Oxford: Clarendon Press, 1965); D. J. McCarthy, *Treaty and Covenant* (Rome: Pontifical Biblical Institute, 1963); G. E. Mendenhall, *Law and Covenant in Israel and the Ancient Near East* (Pittsburgh: The Biblical Colloquium, 1955). However, in recent years less assurance is being voiced about the legitimacy of these parallels [cf. B. S. Childs, "Exodus" in *The Old Testament Library* (Philadelphia: The Westminster Press, 1974), p. 348; J. P. Hyatt, "Exodus" in *The New Century Bible* (London: Oliphants, 1971), pp. 198,99.

commands has been partly responsible for the criticism leveled against the Jewish and Christian faiths that they take all the pleasure out of life by their restrictions. In answer, however, it should be noted that a negative statement always implies the positive ("Thou shalt not steal" could be expressed, "Thou shalt be honest") and that the laws of God were not designed to deny us anything that is really good or to repress us, but are for our well-being and are intended to guide us to the fullest enjoyment of life. If the "thou shalt nots" of the Bible appear to be restrictive, how much more the "thou shalts," e.g., "Thou shalt love the Lord thy God with all thy heart . . . Thou shalt love thy neighbour as thyself (Matt. 22:37,39).

A third characteristic of the Commandments is that they are all expressed in the second person singular (the archaic "thou" of the KJV preserves the singular form which is lost in the "you" of modern English). The use of the singular pronoun may be interpreted as a way of speaking to all Israel in a collective sense (called "corporate personality," i.e., the group thinks and acts as though it were one person), or it may be understood as an emphatic reminder to each individual within the community who heard the law of his responsibility to obey it. The well-being of ancient Israel depended upon the obedience of individuals within the covenant community.

A final characteristic of the form of the Commandments concerns the relationships implied in the commands. The first four commandments deal primarily with the individual's relationship to God (called the vertical relationship) and the remaining six with his relationship to other people (called the horizontal relationship). It is a mistake to emphasize one of these relationships to the exclusion of the other; the result will be an unbalanced expression of one's faith.

A question frequently asked about the Ten Commandments is, "Are Christians obligated to keep the Ten Commandments?" The answer is an unqualified "yes." The spirit of the Commandments is binding even on the person who insists that his salvation is all of grace and not dependent on works. There is a timeless quality in the moral and ethical admonitions contained in these laws; there is not one of them that we can honestly say society or the individual is better off by ignoring. It should also be noted that Jesus said He did not come to abolish the law but to fulfill it (Matt. 5:17). Once He summarized in two statements the manner in which the Old Testament law should be kept (Matt. 22:37-40), and on another occasion He made the same summation in only one statement (Matt. 7:12). The New Testament constantly links the evidence of our love for our Lord with obedience (e.g., Matt. 7:21; John 14:21,23; 1 John 5:3). The fact that the Christian is under grace instead of an Old Testament legal relationship with God should not lead him to conclude that disobedience to God's laws has replaced obedience.

Protestants consider verse 3 as the first commandment, but in Judaism verse 2 is the first, so in order to get the traditional number of ten, verses 3-6 are together counted as the second commandment. Roman Catholics also group verses 3-6 together but call them the first commandment. They divide the tenth (20:17) into two parts to make the required number of ten.

A number of studies have been made of the Ten Commandments,[3] and it would be impossible to include everything that could be written about these "Ten Words." In the following paragraphs each commandment will be considered briefly, including its background, its meaning for Israel, and its contemporary application.

a) *Respect for the uniqueness of God* (20:3). The first commandment, "Thou shalt have no other gods before me," was responsible for shaping the monotheistic faith of Israel. The belief in one God set the Israelite religion apart from all other ancient Near Eastern religions. No other ancient law code has been found that prohibits the worship of other gods. This commandment is basic to all the others, for unless God is unique and the only god, none of the other commandments is binding upon us. "Before me" (literally, "against my face") expresses God's insistence upon undivided allegiance to Him and worship of Him only. Many people, if asked, would deny that they break this commandment, yet violate its spirit and intent, for anything that is more important to them than God becomes their god, whether it be wealth, career, family, or pleasure. Any form of self-exaltation above God is a form of practicing atheism. The New Testament parallel of this commandment is found in John 14:6: "I am the way — the truth and the life. No one comes to the Father except through me" (NIV).

---

[3]The following books are suggested for further study on the Ten Commandments: William Barclay, *The Ten Commandments for Today* (New York: Harper & Row, Publishers, 1973); Joy Davidman, *Smoke on the Mountain* (Philadelphia: Westminster Press, 1953); Roy L. Honeycutt, *These Ten Words* (Nashville: Broadman Press, 1966); G. Campbell Morgan, *The Ten Commandments* (Chicago: Bible Institute Colportage Association of Chicago, 1901); Johann Jakob Stamm and Maurice Edward Andrew, *The Ten Commandments in Recent Research*, Studies in Biblical Theology, Second Series, No. 2 (London: SCM Press, Ltd., 1967); Elton Trueblood, *Foundations for Reconstruction*, rev. ed. (New York: Harper & Row, Publishers, 1961); Ronald S. Wallace, *The Ten Commandments: A Study of Ethical Freedom* (Edinburgh: Oliver and Boyd, 1965); Jay G. Williams, *Ten Words of Freedom* (Philadelphia: Fortress Press, 1971).

b) *Respect for the spiritual nature of God* (20:4-6). The prohibition against making images is not a wholesale condemnation of all art forms but specifically forbids the making of any image, whether of God, man, animal, or plant that might be worshiped as a god. It was given against the background of a world that largely believed the gods could reside in stone or wood representations and that these gods could be controlled to work on behalf of the worshiper if he performed certain rituals or repeated certain incantations. God, however, is sovereign and cannot be controlled by rites or words; He is spirit (John 4:24) and cannot be adequately represented by any likeness nor can He be contained in any one location. The basis of this commandment is that God is a jealous God (Exod. 20:5). Jealousy as used of God in the Old Testament is not the base human emotion that is associated with envy, pettiness, and suspicion; the word would better be translated "zealous." It comes from a word that means "to be red in the face" and is as much part of the nature of God as are His love and forgiveness. It means He really cares for those who give their allegiance to Him, for one cannot be jealous of that to which he is indifferent or feels no attachment. The jealousy of God is the deep emotion He feels when anything or anyone tries to draw our devotion away from Him.

This commandment closes with a sobering reminder of the consequences of one's sins on future generations. "Visiting the iniquity of the fathers upon the children" (20:5) cannot mean that innocent, unborn generations will be punished for the sins of their predecessors (see Deut. 24:16; Jer. 31:29,30; and Ezek. 18:1-4 for the unmistakable statement of the doctrine of individual responsibility). It does mean that future generations can suffer the consequences of the sins of their predecessors because of the unity of the human race (whether it be the consequences of war, drunkenness, drugs, or other forms of immoral behavior). We cannot insist that it is our right to do whatever we desire, because no one can sin without hurting others. Like concentric circles that appear when a stone is thrown in water, so everything we do, whether good or evil, affects countless other lives.

On the other hand, one's devotion to God will result in blessing to thousands (Exod. 20:6). Scholars have debated whether "thousands" means thousands of people or thousands of generations. Hebrew parallelism (with v. 5) would require that "thousands of generations" is the intended meaning. The contrast, therefore, is impressive — the consequences of wicked, godless behavior is felt for several generations, but the influence of devoted, obedient worshipers of God continues for countless generations. The New Testament tells us how to keep this commandment: "God is spirit, and his worshipers must worship in spirit and in truth" (John 4:24, niv).

c) *Respect for the name of God* (20:7). The command, "Thou shalt not take the name of the Lord thy God in vain," usually is associated with profanity or any careless or irreverent use of God's name, but its implications go far beyond this limited interpretation. "In vain" means "groundlessly," "emptily," "without basis," and includes any frivolous, insincere, or unjustified use of God's name. The command may be violated by profanity, by using God's name when there is no genuine faith or commitment (e.g., the politician creating a religious image while seeking votes), or by using God's name to manipulate people (e.g., the preacher who tells his congregation, "*God* wants us to undertake this project," when it really is what the preacher wants). In order to avoid violating this commandment, the ancient Hebrews reasoned that it would be better never to utter the sacred name, "The Lord" (Hebrew, *Yahweh*), and to this day they substitute another name, "Adonai," in its place rather than speak the sacred name. Matthew 5:33-37 says that any kind of swearing is unnecessary; a simple "yes" or "no" is a sufficient answer.

d) *Respect for God's day of rest* (20:8-11). This is one of two commandments stated positively; it begins with the word "Remember" (in the Hebrew language the form of this verb is even more emphatic than a normal imperative). The parallel statement found in Deuteronomy 5:12 begins with "Keep" ("Observe," rsv). "Sabbath" is from a Hebrew word meaning "to cease," "to rest"; it does not come from the word "seven," though the Sabbath was in fact the seventh day of the week in the Hebrew calendar. This passage justifies its observance on the basis of God's rest from His creation activity on the seventh day (20:11); Deuteronomy 5:15, however, makes the observance of the Sabbath a commemoration of the Exodus from Egypt.

Many attempts have been made to find the origin of the Jewish Sabbath in other cultures, particularly in Babylon, where every seventh day (called the *šabattu*) was also a rest day. However, in Babylon those days were regarded as evil days, and therefore it was considered best to do nothing during them. The Sabbath also was observed in Canaan, but again it was totally negative in character, an evil day. In Israel, however, its significance was completely transformed. It became the sign of the covenant (Ezek. 20:12) and a day set aside for joyful worship of God.

In New Testament times overly strict interpretations of the Sabbath were superimposed on it so that the day became burdensome for the people. The Jews developed thirty-nine classifications of work, capable of infinite subdivision, that must be avoided on the Sabbath. It seemed that the best way to avoid violating the Sabbath was to lie perfectly still for twenty-four hours! Jesus tried to restore the original intent of the Sabbath (Matt. 12:5,6,11,12; Mark 3:4; Luke 13:15; John 7:22,23). It was never intended to be a burdensome day upon man, but to be a day of privilege, when every person could live like a king, free from work or obligation to anyone else, a day to renew his physical body through rest and his spiritual being through worship.

e) *Respect for one's parents* (20:12). The fifth commandment is the second command that is stated positively (cf. 20:8) and that also employs an emphatic verb form, "honor" (cf. Lev. 19:3). Society in the ancient world was built around the clan or family. The older members of the family were honored and cared for. The ancients understood the importance of the stability of the home as a prime factor in the stability of the entire society.

The word "honor" comes from a word meaning "to be heavy" and is the same word that frequently is translated "glory." The link between "heavy" and "honor" is understood against the background of the ancient world in which a heavy person was obviously affluent, because only the wealthy had enough to eat. Being wealthy, he was respected and honored by the community. The verse could be translated, "Respect your father and your mother."

The command is unconditional, that is, it is not conditioned on whether the parents deserve respect or not, nor does the child ever reach an age when he no longer is required to respect his parents. In a world that relegated women to an inferior status, it is significant that the mother was to be honored equally with the father in Israel.

Among the reasons given to justify this commandment is the acknowledgment that life is a gift from God and is transmitted through parents. Also, they are God's representatives with delegated authority from God over the children. To dishonor parents, therefore, is to dishonor God. Since parents are God's representatives, the child learns how to honor God by honoring his parents. Evangelists have reported that it is extremely difficult to teach a person to respect God and to believe in Him if that person was not taught when he was a child to respect his parents.

This is the first commandment with a stated promise for those who keep it: "that thy days may be long upon the land" (cf. Eph. 6:2). The obvious meaning of the promise was that Israel would be secure in her possession of the land if she kept this commandment. It has also been understood by some to imply extended years of physical life for the individual who honors his or her parents.

f) *Respect for human life* (20:13). The sixth, seventh, and eighth commandments are expressed in only two words in Hebrew, and to preserve their terseness they could be translated: "no killing, no adultery, no stealing" (20:13-15). The obvious basis for the command not to kill is that man is made in the image and likeness of God (Gen. 1:27) and is, therefore, of infinite value to Him. The command underscores the sanctity of human life. However, it did not serve as a blanket prohibition against all killing, but only against unauthorized killing, the taking of the law into one's own hands. The commandment did not prohibit the death penalty (Gen. 9:6); Israelite law specifically required the taking of the life of an enemy in warfare (Deut. 13:15; 1 Sam. 15:3) and the life of the adulterer (Lev. 20:10). It also permitted a man to inflict blood vengeance on someone who murdered his kinsman (Num. 35:19).

The spirit of this command can be violated by the exploitation of another person, by indifference to human needs, or by destroying the reputation of another. This commandment also figures prominently in the current controversy over abortion and euthanasia. Jesus' interpretation of it is much stricter because He broadens it to include anger with one's brother (Matt. 5:21-26).

g) *Respect for marriage* (20:14). Marriage is a covenant relationship between two people which places certain obligations upon both parties, especially a pledge of faithfulness one to the other. This commandment requires purity of the marriage state. Adultery violates the marriage trust and shows a fundamental disrespect for one's mate. Two factors are necessary if this commandment is to be kept: (1) respect for the sanctity of the marriage relationship, both one's own and the marriage of others; and (2) a commitment to personal purity and sexual expression only within the confines of marriage. The best way for a Christian to deal with this temptation is to remember that his body has been joined to the body of Christ (1 Cor. 6:19,20; Gal. 2:20; Col. 1:27). Therefore, because Christ dwells within him, his body cannot belong to anyone else (outside of marriage) and to Christ.

Jesus' interpretation of this commandment was even more stern than its Old Testament application; He said that the lustful look violates the spirit of the command (Matt. 5:27-30). Historians are warning today's permissive society that the past has shown that the strength and stability of a society are dependent upon the stability of the marriage relationship.

h) *Respect for the property of others* (20:15). The Bible defends the right to hold property. The possession of property in itself is not evil; what one does with his possessions or what they do to him may be evil. What a person possesses represents in tangible form how he has invested his time and life, and because life is sacred, whatever represents that life is also sacred. The Bible defends the right to own property but not to the extent that others would be injured or oppressed by one's pursuit of possessions (cf. Amos 2:7; 4:1; 6:1-6). The Old Testament contains laws prohibiting the stealing of people (Exod. 21:16) as well as property (22:1-4). It also says that withholding tithes and offerings is robbing God (Mal. 3:8-10).

The spirit of this commandment can be broken in ways other than taking the property of another violently or covertly. The employee who takes paper clips, postage stamps, stationery, etc., from his employer for personal use, the taxpayer who falsifies his tax return, the friend who borrows money or even a cup of sugar without intent of returning it, the shopkeeper who uses dishonest scales or engages in any kind of fraudulent business practice, the student who takes credit for work that was done by someone else, the employee who loafs on the job but accepts full wages, or the nation that takes the land of another by war — all violate this commandment. Stated positively in the New Testament, this commandment gives us the freedom to share our possessions freely with others (Luke 6:38; Eph. 4:28).

i) *Respect for truth and the honor of others* (20:16). The command not to bear false witness against one's neighbor originated in the setting of the court where witnesses were under oath to tell the truth, but in its broader application it is a prohibition against untruthfulness of any kind (cf. Lev. 19:11, which specifically forbids lying, and Hos. 4:2, which equates this command with lying). A false witness could bring about the death of an innocent person (1 Kings 21:10,13; Matt. 26:59-61) or destroy the reputation of another person (Deut. 19:16-19). The seriousness of this sin lies in the fact that an attack on another person is an attack against God, for man is created in the image of God, and God is jealous for His creation. The tongue is a powerful weapon (cf. James 3:5,6); it can destroy as surely as killing does, whether it is the malicious lie, idle gossip, propaganda, or a half-truth. Insincere flattery, even the raised eyebrow, or keeping silent when another's reputation is being unjustly maligned violate the spirit of this command. The New Testament counterpart of the ninth command is to speak the truth in love (Eph. 4:15; cf. Eph. 4:25; 6:14).

j) *Respect for the power of thoughts* (20:17). At first glance the command not to covet anything that belongs to someone else might not seem to be as important as some of the others, because no damage actually is done to the neighbor, since it involves only a thought. However, the very inwardness of the command that forbids a wrong attitude toward another reveals that the root of every sin committed against other people begins with the thought, for the thought is father to the act. Covetousness is the most basic cause of human strife and misery (James 4:2). The great lie of covetousness is the belief that the attainment of what we desire inordinately will bring happiness. Some Old Testament people who learned that coveting leads to disastrous consequences were Eve (forbidden fruit, Gen. 3:6), King Ahab (Naboth's vineyard, 1 Kings 21), and David (Uriah's wife, 2 Sam. 11:2-21).

The Hebrew word for covet *(hamad)* is in itself a neutral word that means "desire," "take pleasure in." It is only when desire is directed into wrong channels — wanting something that belongs to another, something to which we have no right — that it becomes wrong. Not all coveting, however, is wrong! "Covet earnestly the best gifts" (1 Cor. 12:31; cf. Ps. 19:10). The New Testament remedy for dealing with covetousness is to "be content with what you have" (Heb. 13:5, NIV). It also warns that covetousness is as serious a sin as idolatry (Eph. 5:5; cf. 1 Cor. 5:10).

It has been said facetiously, "The eleventh commandment is, 'Thou shalt not get caught.'" Some have the attitude that anything is all right as long as one gets away with the deed, but no one can really break the moral laws of God, for they are so built into the warp and woof of life that we discover too late we have only broken ourselves on God's laws. The Ten Commandments have proved to be a durable guide for the most basic interpersonal relationships of life. Their influence on Western law and morality has been incalculable.

B. The People's Fear of God (20:18-21)

When the people saw the lightning and smoke on the mountain and heard the thunder and sound of the trumpet, they were terrified and begged Moses to speak to them, instead of God; they were afraid they might die if God spoke directly to them. They said, "We will hear" (20:19), which is equivalent in Hebrew to saying, "We will obey," as the Hebrew language does not have different words to express these two ideas. The Israelites knew that hearing the voice of God required that they obey Him. Moses allayed their fears and explained that God had come to prove them, that is, to see if they would really obey God as they said they would (20:20; a frequent theme of the Old Testament; 15:25; 16:4; Deut. 8:2; Judg. 2:22; Ps. 81:7).

For Further Study

1. In a Bible dictionary or encyclopedia (see bibliography) read articles on law in the ancient Near East, Sinai, covenant, the Ten Commandments.

2. What is the difference between a covenant of law and a covenant of grace?

3. Which of the Ten Commandments are binding on Christians? Justify your answer.

4. Make a study of the covenants in the Old Testament. How many different covenants may be identified?

5. What do chapters 19:1–20:21 teach about the nature of God?

6. Make a study of law codes of the ancient Near East and compare them with the Mosaic code. What similarities and what differences did you discover?

Chapter 8

The Covenant at Sinai. II: Civil, Criminal, and Ceremonial Law

(Exodus 20:22–24:18)

Following the Ten Commandments a number of laws dealing largely with civil and criminal matters was given to Israel. This section of Exodus usually is called the Book of the Covenant and takes its name from 24:7. The laws deal with such matters as slaves, injury to person, property rights, and moral and religious duties. In contrast to the ancient law code of Hammurabi that placed a higher value on property rights than on human rights, these laws elevate human life to a level above material values. They reduce the gross brutality of punishment inflicted on guilty persons under other ancient law codes and reject preferential treatment for some people in the administration of justice. The penalty for violation of the laws was death, a fine, restitution, or punishment that was imposed immediately; the law did not provide for stated terms of imprisonment as a form of punishment.

A. The Book of the Covenant (20:22–23:33)

1. *Instructions for acceptable worship* (20:22-26)

God told Moses to instruct the people not to make idols of gold or silver as a means of worshiping Him but to make an altar of earth (though later the altars were much more elaborate), where they would sacrifice their burnt offerings and peace offerings (20:23,24). The burnt offering consisted of an animal that was completely consumed in the fire (cf. Lev. 1:3-17), whereas the peace offering was partly consumed in the fire and partly a meal shared by the priest and the offerer (cf. Lev. 3:1-17). The peace offering signified mutual peace and friendship with God and those with whom the meal was shared. The people were further instructed not to use hewn stone if they made an altar of stone, because a tool (20:25; literally, "sword") used to cut the stone would profane it. The meaning of this prohibition has been variously understood. Some trace it back to primitive times when the stone was believed to be the abode of the deity, who would be driven out by the blows of the tool. Others understand it as an expression of the simplicity of worship that God desired from His people, while others have noted that the sword was a symbol of strife, whereas the altar was a symbol of reconciliation (cf. God's rejection of David as the temple builder because he had shed blood, 1 Chron. 28:3).

As further evidence of the sanctity of the altar and as a rebuke of any careless conduct while worshiping, God warned the people not to go up to the altar by steps in order that their nakedness would not be exposed (20:26). "Nakedness" is a frequent Old Testament euphemism for the sexual organs (cf. Lev. 18:6). Ritual nakedness was a common feature of early cults, but it was not to be tolerated in Israel. In summary, acceptable worship of God required that there be no idolatry, no ostentation, and no careless or disrespectful conduct. The New Testament equivalent of this command is given in 1 Corinthians 14:33, 40.

2. Laws concerning Hebrew slaves (21:1-11)

Human slavery was a way of life in the ancient world. Slaves were looked upon as property and had no rights. The Mosaic law represented an advancement in the struggle for human rights, as it provided some safeguards for slaves. The law given here is concerned only with Hebrew slaves; foreign slaves are dealt with in Leviticus 25:44-46. An Israelite could be sold by his parents, a practice particularly common with daughters. A person could be sold for stealing if unable to make restitution (22:3) or to pay debts (2 Kings 4:1; cf. 1 Sam. 22:2; Neh. 5:1-5). A poverty-stricken Israelite could sell himself as a slave (Lev. 25:39; Deut. 15:12-17), but no Israelite could be held as a slave for more than six years (21:2).

At the end of his servitude a man was to leave his master's service exactly as he entered it. If single when enslaved, he went out single (literally, "with his body," an unusual expression found only here and in 21:4). If married (21:3; literally, "master or owner of a woman," the usual Hebrew way of referring to marriage), his wife went with him at the end of the period of enslavement. If the owner gave him a wife and she bore him children, both the wife and children would belong to the owner at the end of the enslavement. However, if a man chose to remain enslaved for life because of his love for his master, his wife, and his children, he was allowed to make that decision. The master would take him to the door (it is not certain whether the door of the sanctuary or the door of the master's house was intended) and pierce his ear with an awl, either as a symbol of attachment to that household or as a symbol of obedience (cf. Deut. 15:16,17).

A man's daughter sold as a slave was not automatically freed at the end of six years, however (21:7). If she did not please her master, she could not be sold to a foreigner, but her family or clan was allowed to redeem her. If the girl was given to the master's son, she had to be treated as a daughter, fully protected as a wife, even if the son took another wife. If any of her rights were violated, she was to be freed without reimbursement (21:11).

In answer to critics of the laws regarding slavery in the Old Testament, it should be said that the Bible approves slavery only in the same way it does divorce (cf. Deut. 24:1-4; Mal. 2:15,16; Matt. 19:3-9; Mark 10:2-9); people were going to traffic in slavery anyway, so the laws were established to give some kind of protection to the one enslaved.

3. *Laws governing death or injury to a person* (21:12-32)

The Mosaic law provided the death penalty for stated crimes (cf. Gen. 9:6). Premeditated murder required the death penalty (Exod. 21:12,14), whereas the person who killed another by accident was provided a place of safety where he could flee (21:13; some think the altar is meant here, cf. 1 Kings 1:50-53; 2:28,29; but the verse more likely anticipates the cities of refuge, cf. Num. 35:6-15; Deut. 19:1-10; Josh. 20:1-6). Other crimes that invoked the death penalty were striking one's father or mother (Exod. 21:15; a reminder of the high respect given to parents in ancient times), stealing another person, whether the thief sold him as a slave or not (21:16; cf. Amos 1:6,9; 2:6), and cursing one's parents (Exod. 21:17; cf. Deut. 21:18-21). There was no death penalty for the person who killed his slave, for the slave was looked upon as a man's property (Exod. 21:20,21).

There were other crimes not punishable by death but which required some kind of restitution. If a man injured another in a fight, he was required to pay for the loss of his time and to see that he was thoroughly healed (21:18,19). If two men fighting caused a pregnant woman to miscarry, the one responsible for her injury was required to pay a fine (21:22). The summary of the laws regarding restitution are found in 21:23-25 (" . . . eye for eye, tooth for tooth . . ."; cf. Matt. 5:38-42 for Jesus' interpretation of this law). This type of law usually is referred to as the Lex Talionis, or law of retaliation. It was not a vestige from a more primitive age or a backward step in the administration of justice, though it has been frequently interpreted as vengeful and cruel. It actually represented an improvement over previous laws, for it limited punishment to an exact equivalent so that the punishment would not be out of proportion to the crime, e.g., an eye, but no more than an eye (cf. Shylock's demand for a pound of flesh in Shakespeare's *The Merchant of Venice*). It also put the rich and nobility under the same law as the poor and the commoner. The wealthy could not escape punishment for their crimes simply by paying a fine. As evidence of the protection afforded slaves, who in most ancient societies had no protection under the law against the violence of their masters, Israelite law went a step beyond the "eye for an eye" principle. If a man struck a slave and blinded him or knocked out a tooth, the slave was to be set free (21:26,27).

Further evidence of the sanctity of human life in Israelite law is demonstrated in the law that required the killing of an ox that gored someone to death (21:28). However, if the ox was known to be dangerous but the owner had taken no measures to restrain it, then not only would the animal be killed but its owner also would be put to death (21:29), unless the relatives of the victim were willing to accept monetary compensation for his life (21:30). If the ox gored a slave, monetary restitution of thirty shekels of silver was given (the purchase price of a slave), and the animal would be killed, but there was no provision for killing the owner of the animal (21:32).

4. *Laws governing damage to property* (21:33–22:15)

There were other provisions for restitution for loss of livestock or other property, whether through carelessness (21:33-36; 22:5,6), through theft (22:1-4), or through breach of trust of goods or animals kept for another (22:7-13), or of anything borrowed (22:14,15).

5. *Other moral and ritual laws* (22:16–23:19)

a) *Regarding seduction* (22:16,17). If a man seduced a maiden who was not betrothed, he was required to pay the marriage price (Hebrew, *mohar,* found only two other times in the Old Testament, Gen. 34:12; 1 Sam. 18:25). The *mohar* was not a dowry but the purchase price of a wife; however, it was considered not so much a price paid for the woman as compensation for anticipated loss of income the daughter would have brought to the family. Fifty shekels of silver was the specified amount that had to be paid (Deut. 22:29). However, if the father refused to give his violated daughter in marriage, the offender still was obligated to pay the marriage price (Exod. 22:17), as her loss of virginity would reduce the amount of money the father could receive for her when she married.

b) *Regarding capital offenses* (22:18-20). Three crimes punishable by death are enumerated in these verses (cf. 21:12-17,29 for other capital offenses): sorcery, bestiality, and idolatrous sacrifice. The sorceress (22:18; from a word "to cut") was one who claimed supernatural powers through the control of or assistance of divine powers (cf. Deut. 18:9-14; Isa. 47:9-12; Jer. 27:9; Ezek. 13:9; Mic. 5:12); this verse was used to justify the punishment of witches in New England in colonial times. Bestiality (Exod. 22:19), though common in the ancient world, was looked upon with horror in Israel because it was a perversion of the function of sex as given by God and also a debasement of a human being created in the image and likeness of God (cf. Lev. 18:23; 20:15,16; Deut. 27:21). The one who offered sacrifices to other gods was to be utterly destroyed (Exod. 22:20; literally, "put under the ban," a practice frequently mentioned in the Old Testament, e.g., Num. 31:15-17; Deut. 7:2; 20:16,17; Josh. 6:21; 10:11; 11:12; Judg. 21:11; 1 Sam. 15:3; 27:9-11; Jer. 25:9). The worship of other deities was the most serious sin of all in the Old Testament; there was no hope for the individual or nation that would not give up its gods and return to the Lord (Ezek. 18:31).

c) *Humane duties* (22:21-27). The Old Testament shows compassion and concern for the oppressed and unfortunate not found anywhere else in the ancient world. Foreigners, widows, orphans, and the poor were objects of special concern, especially of the prophets (Deut. 10:18; 14:29; 24:17; 26:13; Ps. 68:5; Isa. 1:17; Jer. 7:6; 22:3; Hos. 14:3; Zech. 7:10). God reminded the Israelites not to oppress (Exod. 22:21; literally, "push, press"; KJV, "vex") strangers (22:21; literally, "resident aliens"), remembering the treatment they had endured as strangers in Egypt (cf. Deut. 10:19). Furthermore, widows and orphans were not to be mistreated, upon pain of severe punishment of the offenders (Exod. 22:22-24).

Another group of people for whom God provided safeguards were the poor who might be forced to borrow money from a neighbor. The poor were not to be charged interest (22:25; "usury," KJV; from a word "to bite"; cf. Neh. 5:3-10; Deut. 23:20). The garment taken in pledge for a loan was to be returned each evening before sunset, as it might be the only covering a poor man had against the cold Palestinian nights (cf. Amos 2:8; Ezek. 18:12,16; Job 22:6).

d) *Duties to God* (22:28-31). Evey Israelite had certain obligations to God under the covenant; four of them are given in these verses. First, he must not revile God (22:28; the Hebrew word *qalal* used here is practically synonymous with the other word in the same verse, '*arar,* that also means "curse"). The KJV says "revile the gods," but this translation is unlikely and would contradict the attitude toward other gods found everywhere else in the Old Testament. The Hebrew word is *elohim,* a plural word which sometimes can be translated "gods" (e.g., Gen. 31:30; 35:2; Deut. 4:28; Judg. 2:3), but is used 2570 times in the Old Testament to mean God. The command is extended also to include the people's ruler (Exod. 22:28; literally, "one lifted up"), for the authority given to the ruler came from God (cf. Rom. 13:1-7).

The second duty imposed on the Israelites was the injunction not to delay in bringing the offerings to God from the abundance of their harvests (Exod. 22:29a). They also were reminded again concerning their duty to give the firstborn to God (22:29b,30; see discussion at 13:1-16). This verse has been cited as proof that human sacrifice was lawfully practiced in the earlier part of Israel's history, but this interpretation contradicts God's abhorrence of human sacrifice that is found everywhere else in the Old Testament.

The final duty to God in this section emphasizes the necessity of being separated (22:31; "holy," KJV). One way they could show their consecration to God was by not eating any flesh that had been torn by wild animals. The basis of this prohibition might have been that the blood from the flesh was not properly drained (cf. Lev. 17:10,11; Deut. 12:16,23), or perhaps it was for health reasons; such flesh would doubtless have been contaminated and not fit for human consumption.

e) *The practice of justice* (23:1-9). These verses contain a number of unrelated regulations, all of which demonstrate the spirit in which justice was to be administered by the Israelites. Several of these laws have already been given, though in slightly different words (e.g., cf.

23:1a with 20:16; cf. 23:9 with 22:21). Justice was to be administered impartially; not even the poor man was to be favored (23:3). An incipient New Testament doctrine, "Love your enemies" (Matt. 5:44) is found in 23:4,5 with its injunction to return an enemy's straying animal to him and to help that animal when it falls under a heavy load. The Israelite was not to take a bribe (23:8, translated as "gift" in the KJV, for "gift" in Old English could mean "bribe"), because it would make it difficult for officials receiving the bribes to render impartial justice.

f) *Seventh year, Sabbath, and sacred feasts* (23:10-19). The sacred seasons and feasts were an important part of the expression of the faith of Israel. However, they were not always carefully observed (Neh. 13:18; Ezek. 20:13; Hos. 2:13; Mal. 1:6,7,13), and even when they were, the spirit in which the offering was brought was often wrong, and therefore the offering itself was unacceptable to God (Isa. 1:12-17; Hos. 2:11-17; Amos 5:21; 8:10). Exodus 23:10-19 mentions some of the most important sacred seasons and festivals that were enjoined upon the Israelites by God.

The first of the sacred seasons in these verses was the Sabbath of the seventh year (23:10,11). Every seventh year the Israelites were required to let their land lie fallow. Even that which grew of itself was not to be gathered by the owner but was left for the poor. The ostensible motive for this regulation seemed to be humanitarian — food for the poor — but it also incorporated a scientific principle of agriculture that has been "discovered" in modern times — crop rotation to prevent soil depletion. It would have taken a great deal of faith on the part of the average Israelite to keep this law, and since so many of the other laws were violated, it is highly unlikely that this one was conscientiously observed (cf. 2 Chron. 36:21).

The second of the sacred seasons included in these verses was the Sabbath. It is a repetition of the law already given in 20:8-11 (see discussion there), but does add the fact that the purpose of the Sabbath was to give a time of refreshment (23:12; from a word meaning "to breathe") to animals, slaves, and strangers.

Each year Israelite males (23:17) were required to keep three feasts (23:14; from a word that means a feast accompanied by a pilgrimage; see discussion at 5:1-9). The first of these was Unleavened Bread (23:15; probably intended to include the Passover; see discussion at 12:14-20). The second was the Feast of Harvest (23:16), a term found only here. Elsewhere this festival is referred to as Firstfruits (Lev. 23:10; Num.

28:26; Deut. 18:4), the time of year when the firstfruits of the harvest were presented as offerings to God. It also was known as the Feast of Weeks (Hebrew, *Shevuoth*, 34:22; Deut. 16:10) or Pentecost (Acts 2:1, from a Greek word meaning "fiftieth") and was celebrated fifty days after the Feast of Unleavened Bread (Deut. 16:9,10). The third festival was the Feast of Ingathering (23:16), which was observed at the end of the year after the harvest had been gathered in. This festival was better known as the Feast of Tabernacles (Lev. 23:34; Deut. 16:13) or Booths (Hebrew, *Sukkoth*, Lev. 23:42; Neh. 8:14). These three festivals still are observed in Judaism.

With regard to the sacrifices, the people were instructed not to offer the blood of the sacrifice with leavened bread or to allow the fat of the animal sacrifice to remain until morning (23:18; cf. Lev. 3:17). The section closes with a regulation that seems somewhat strange and has occasioned a number of interpretations: "Thou shalt not seethe ("boil," RSV) a kid in his mother's milk" (23:19b). Some have attributed it to a humanitarian motive or a repudiation of gluttony, but it more likely finds its origin in a Canaanite fertility rite, in which a kid was cooked in milk, after which the fields were sprinkled with the pieces of the cooked animal in order to insure the fertility of the soil and abundant crops. This law, then, would be a repudiation of a practice that was associated with the Canaanite cult.

6. *Guidance promised on the way to Canaan* (23:20-33)

The Book of the Covenant concludes with God's promise to send His angel before His people to guard them and to lead them into the Promised Land (23:20). The angel of the Lord cannot be separated from God Himself and must be understood as a manifestation of God, "for my name is in him" (23:21; see further discussion at 3:1-6). If the people would be obedient, God would drive out the native Amorite, Hittite, Perizzite, Canaanite, Hivite, and Jebusite inhabitants of the land (23:23). The people were warned not to worship the native deities but to destroy them completely, along with their sacred pillars (symbols of the deity). In return for their obedience God promised to bless them with food, health, many offspring, and long life (23:25,26).

God also promised to drive out the inhabitants of the land before His people, sending upon them fear (23:27) and hornets (23:28; meaning is uncertain; perhaps it is a reference to plagues, an enemy, or is a metaphor describing God's activity on behalf of His people; cf. Deut.

7:20; Josh. 24:12 for the only other occurrences of the word). However, God said He would not drive the people out in one year because the Israelites would not be numerous enough to occupy and take care of the land. It would become desolate, and wild animals would become a threat to the Israelites (23:29,30). God would gradually give them the land, as they were able to possess it, from the Mediterranean (23:31; literally, "sea of the Philistines") to the Euphrates (23:31; literally, "unto the river"). He concluded His promise of victory with a solemn warning not to make a covenant with the native inhabitants or to worship their gods or to allow them to remain in the land, lest the Israelites be enticed to worship their gods. Unfortunately, the people did not heed this warning. They did not drive the Canaanites out of the land but settled down among them and worshiped the Canaanite deities, thereby bringing upon themselves the destruction of their nation.

B. Ratification of the Covenant (24:1-18)

Upon hearing the terms of the covenant God was willing to make with them, it was now Israel's turn to accept or reject the covenant, the heart of which was the obligation to obey God's laws in order to be the recipients of His blessings. Chapter 24 with its account of the ratification of the covenant could well be called the climax of the Book of Exodus (cf. Heb. 9;10, especially 9:18-21, which uses this scene as the prototype of the ratification of the New Covenant).

1. Ratification by the people (24:1-11)

When Moses returned to the people and told them all the provisions the Lord had laid down for the covenant, they ratified it by responding with one accord, "All the words which the LORD hath said will we do" (24:3). Moses wrote down the Lord's words (another reminder that Moses was a highly literate man, cf. 17:14; 34:28) and the next day built an altar and erected twelve pillars as a symbol of the twelve tribes of Israel. He sent young men to offer burnt offerings and peace offerings to the Lord (the priesthood had not yet been established to have charge of the sacrifices). Then Moses took half the blood of the sacrificial animals and put it in basins and sprinkled the other half on the altar to symbolize the ratification of the covenant (and perhaps to symbolize forgiveness).

Other ways that covenants were sealed in the ancient Near East included eating salt together (Lev. 2:13; Num. 18:19), eating a sacrificial meal together (Gen. 31:54), exchanging articles of clothing (1 Sam. 18:1-4), and walking between the divided pieces of a slaughtered animal (Gen. 15:10,17). In the blood ritual (whether by sprinkling, tasting, or smearing blood on one's body), the two parties were considered to be organically united into a sacred bond. The shedding of blood played a decisive role in other biblical covenants, such as the covenant with Abraham that required circumcision (Gen. 17:9-14) and the establishment of the New Covenant (Matt. 26:28; 1 Cor. 11:25; Heb. 9:22).

Moses read aloud the words of the covenant he had recorded (24:7), and again they gave their assent, whereupon he took the blood and sprinkled it on the people, thereby symbolically joining them to the covenant.

After this, Moses, together with Aaron, Aaron's sons Nadab and Abihu, and seventy of the elders of Israel ascended the mountain where they saw God. Under His feet was a pavement of transparent sapphire stone (24:10, perhaps lapis lazuli; cf. Isa. 6:1,2 and Ezek. 1:22-28 for the closest parallels to this awesome revelation of the divine glory), and there on the mountain they joined in a covenant meal.

2. Ratification by the appearance of God on Sinai (24:12-18)

Then God instructed Moses to come up into the mountain where He would give him the law written on tables of stone (24:12). Moses left Aaron and Hur to settle any differences among the people that might arise while he was gone and then took Joshua with him to the mountain of God. A cloud covered the mountain, and the glory of the Lord settled on it (literally, "dwelt"; the word "shekinah" comes from the same word; thus the "shekinah glory" is the dwelling glory or the presence of God). The glory of the Lord was like a devouring fire on top of the mountain and visible even to the Israelites below. The cloud remained six days, and then on the seventh day God called to Moses out of the cloud. Moses thereupon entered the cloud and remained on the mountain forty days and forty nights communing with God.

For Further Study

1. In a Bible dictionary or encyclopedia (see bibliography) read articles on Sabbath, slavery, blood, Feast of Firstfruits (Feast of Weeks), Feast of Tabernacles.

2. What does Exodus 20:22–24:18 teach about the nature of God?

3. Are the Old Testament regulations that demand the death penalty still binding on contemporary society?

4. Make a study of the Old Testament concept of justice and determine its influence on today's legal system.

5. What are some important differences between the New Covenant and the covenant God made with Israel at Sinai?

Chapter 9

Instructions for the Tabernacle and Priests

(Exodus 25:1–31:18)

No other single aspect of Israel's faith is given quite as much attention in the Old Testament as the tabernacle and all that is associated with it. The Book of Exodus devotes seven chapters (25-31) to a description of its specifications and then six more (35-40) that repeat almost word for word the instructions from 25-31 as they were carried out. One scholar has observed that God created the world in six days but took forty days to explain to Moses how to build the tabernacle! Apart from Exodus it is mentioned frequently in the Book of Numbers, but surprisingly, it rarely is mentioned in the rest of the Old Testament, and outside the Book of Hebrews it is referred to only a few times in the New Testament. The tabernacle was replaced by a magnificent temple of stone, wood, and precious metals during the reign of Solomon, but the essential pattern of worship established at Sinai remained unchanged. The tabernacle served as a visible symbol of God's presence in the midst of His people. Its influence on Israel's faith and her understanding of her relationship with God cannot be overstated.

A. The Tabernacle (25:1–27:21)

1. Materials given by the people (25:1-9)

One of the most important phases of a building project is the assembling of materials that will be needed in its construction. At first glance it would seem unlikely that the Israelites, a group of slaves so recently escaped from Egypt and now in a barren wasteland, could acquire some of the materials necessary for the construction of the tabernacle (Hebrew, *mishkan*, a word that means "dwelling place"). But God had already anticipated this problem when He instructed the people to ask the Egyptians for their jewels of gold and silver before their departure (11:2). He told Moses to instruct the people to bring an offering (25:2; Hebrew, *terumah*, a portion that is separated from a larger quantity for sacred purposes). These offerings were to come only from those who gave "willingly with his heart" (25:2; literally, "whose heart urges him"). The amount to be given was left to the individual, but it is a consistent principle throughout the Bible that God wants our service and gifts to be given willingly, never out of a sense of duty (cf. 1 Chron. 29:5; 1 Cor. 9:17; 2 Cor. 9:7; Philem. 14; 1 Peter 5:2).

The people were asked to bring gold, silver, and bronze (25:3). The gold would be used to gild the ark, to make the mercy seat, cherubim, the table of shewbread and its vessels, the lampstand and its equipment, the altar of incense, and various rims, clasps for curtains, frames, and parts of the priestly garments. The silver was for sockets of frames, pedestals, pillars, and hooks; and the bronze (not "brass," KJV, because the alloy of copper and zinc we call brass was not known at that time, whereas bronze, a mixture of copper and tin, was widely used among the ancients) was for the altar of burnt offering and its utensils, the laver, and various pedestals, and clasps for curtains.

They were further instructed to bring fabrics of blue, purple, and scarlet, fine-twined linen (each thread twisted from many strands), goats' hair (usual material for making nomads' tents), rams' skins, badgers' skins (25:5; "goatskins," RSV, though recent studies have identified the skins as a specially finished leather, perhaps of dolphin skins, or it may have been a word for leather in general), and acacia wood ("shittim," KJV; a gnarled and thorny tree that provided a close-grained and durable wood). Many books and articles have been written that offer explanations of the symbolism of the metals and the colors used in the tabernacle, e.g., gold represents divine glory, silver represents redemption, and bronze represents judgment; blue is the heavenly color, purple is the color of royalty, and scarlet represents sacrifice. There is no unanimity of opinion, however, concerning the significance of the metals and colors; and the Old Testament itself does not spell out the symbolism, so it must remain an open question.

Other materials the people were to bring included oil for the lamps, spices for the anointing oil and for the sweet (fragrant) incense, onyx stones (Hebrew, *shoham;* exact identity uncertain but is a precious stone that has been identified as carnelian or lapis lazuli), and other stones for the ephod and the breastpiece of the priestly garments (25:6, 7).

God told Moses that all these materials were to be used to make a sanctuary (literally, "holy place"; see discussion at 15:17) according to the exact instructions that He would give him (a reminder that God alone determines what is acceptable worship), and that it would serve as His dwelling place in their midst.

2. The ark of the covenant (25:10-22)

The single most important piece of furniture in the tabernacle was the ark of the covenant (also called "the ark," 25:14; "the ark of the LORD," 1 Sam. 4:6; "the ark of God," 1 Sam. 4:18; "the ark of the testimony," Exod. 25:22; "the ark of the covenant of God," Judg. 20:27; "the ark of the Lord GOD," 1 Kings 2:26; altogether there are at least twenty-two ways of referring to the ark in the Old Testament). It is not related to the Hebrew word used for Noah's ark (Gen. 6:14) or Moses' ark (Exod. 2:3). The ark represented the presence of God in a very special way, for God promised that He would appear in a cloud upon the mercy seat which was on the ark in the most holy place; there the high priest would enter once a year to sprinkle blood on the mercy seat to atone for the sins of the people (Lev. 16).

The ark was an oblong chest of acacia wood overlaid with pure gold inside and out with an ornamental gold molding around it. It was two and one-half cubits in length and one and one-half cubits in width and height (Exod. 25:10). Exact equivalents cannot be determined since the cubit measurement in ancient times varied from seventeen to twenty-one inches and was based on the distance from the elbow to the tip of the middle finger. A golden ring was attached at each corner through which poles made of acacia wood overlaid with gold were passed that were never to be removed from the rings. The ark was transported by means of the poles (25:12-15; cf. 1 Kings 8:8); the ark itself was never to be touched (cf. 1 Sam. 6:19; 2 Sam. 6:6,7). The tables of the law ("the testimony"; see comment at Exod. 16:31-36) would be placed in the ark (25:16,21).

The mercy seat was to be made of a slab of solid gold the same length and width as the ark and placed on top of it as a cover (25:17,21). "Mercy seat" comes from a word that means "to cover," hence, "to provide reconciliation, atonement." It is from the same word used in Genesis 6:14 to describe the pitch used to cover Noah's ark. The mercy seat was the most sacred object in the tabernacle, for it was the throne of God. Because God spoke from immediately above the mercy seat and from between the two cherubim, it was sometimes called His footstool (Ps. 99:5).

Two cherubim fashioned of gold were to be placed, one at either end of the ark, and fastened securely to it. Their wings were spread out, and they faced each other with their faces toward the mercy seat (Exod. 25:18-20; cf. 2 Chron. 3:10-13 for a description of the cherubim placed in Solomon's temple). "Cherub" (plural, "cherubim") is from a word meaning "intercessor." The cherubim were in the shape of winged animals with human faces and served as guardians of a sacred spot (cf. Gen. 3:24) and as transporters of the deity (Ps. 18:10; Ezek. 1:15-28; 10:15,16). They always are associated with the nearness of God in the Old Testament.

The ark and the cherubim were placed behind the veil in the part of the tabernacle called the Holy of Holies, and were the only articles in that sacred area.

3. *Table of the Bread of the Presence* (25:23-30)

A table was to be made of acacia wood two cubits long, one cubit wide, and a cubit and a half high, overlaid with pure gold, with a molding of gold around it (25:23,24). A rim (25:25; "frame," rsv) a handbreadth wide was put around the table with a decorative molding of gold about the rim. Rings were fastened to each of its corners into which poles of acacia wood overlaid with gold were fitted to carry the table (25:26-28). The dishes and bowls for the table were to be made of pure gold (25:29). The table was put in the holy place on the north side (26:35). Some idea of the appearance of the table may be gained from the Arch of Titus in Rome on which are shown various objects taken by the Romans from Jerusalem in A.D. 70, including the table, though we cannot be sure that the table in Herod's temple was in every detail like the table constructed for the tabernacle.

Loaves of bread, called the Bread of the Presence, always were supposed to be kept on the table. The traditional translation, "shewbread" (literally, "bread of the face," that is, bread placed before the face of God) was first used by Tyndale in 1526 (borrowed from Martin Luther's translation, *Schaubrot*), but it is not the best translation. Twelve loaves of bread were set out in the presence of God every Sabbath (Lev. 24:5-9; cf. 1 Sam. 21:1-6, where the bread was given to David and his soldiers to eat). They were arranged in two rows of six loaves each and perhaps originally symbolized an offering of food to Him, but today there is no agreement about the symbolic meaning. It has been understood by some to be an acknowledgment that God is the provider of our food, and christologically, it has been understood to symbolize Christ as the Bread of Life. In 1 Chronicles 9:32 a different term is used that could be translated literally "bread laid out in rows," but the KJV makes no distinction and calls it "shewbread." It is called "holy bread" ("hallowed bread," KJV) in 1 Samuel 21:4,6.

Leviticus 24:5 says that each loaf of bread was to contain two-tenths of an ephah of fine flour ("two tenth deals," KJV), which would be about seven quarts of flour. Each loaf, therefore, must have been quite large.

4. *The lampstand* (25:31-40)

Next God gave instructions to Moses for making a lampstand ("candlestick," KJV; called the menorah by Jews) of pure gold with six branches going out its sides that together with the central shaft would provide space for seven lamps (25:37). On each branch there were to be three cups in the form of an almond flower, each with capital and flower (25:33) and on the central shaft four cups with their capitals and flowers (25:34). Tongs for adjusting the wick and snuffers ("trays," RSV) were to be made of pure gold (25:38). The lampstand was placed on the south side of the holy place, opposite the table for the Bread of the Presence (26:35). Functionally, its purpose was to illuminate the holy place. Symbolically, it has been interpreted as God's presence in the midst of His people, as Israel shining with the light of truth (cf. Isa. 42:6), or as Christ as the light of the world. The seven-branched menorah from Herod's temple is depicted on the Arch of Titus in Rome and probably was similar in appearance, though not identical, to the lampstand in the tabernacle.

The altar of incense was the third furnishing in the holy place, but it is not described until Exodus 30:1-10.

5. *Architecture of the tabernacle* (26:1-37)

The description of the tabernacle given in chapter 26 is not easy to visualize; therefore, it is helpful to have a drawing of the tabernacle to look at as the chapter is read.[1] The entire tabernacle plan was designed

---

[1] For studies on the tabernacle see: Frank M. Cross, "The Priestly Tabernacle," *Biblical Archaeologist*, X (September 1947): 45-68; *Hastings' Dictionary of the Bible*, 1902 ed., s.v. "Tabernacle," by A.R.S. Kennedy; *Interpreter's Dictionary of the Bible*, 1962 ed., s.v. "Tabernacle," by G. Henton Davies; Moshe Levine, *The Tabernacle: Its Structure and Utensils* (Tel Aviv: Melechet Hamishkan for the Soncino Press, Ltd., 1969); *The Zondervan Pictorial Encyclopedia of the Bible*, 1975, s.v. "Tabernacle" by C. Feinberg.

to show that God dwelt among His people but was separated from them by His holiness and that He could be approached only in ways stipulated by Him.

a) *The curtains* (26:1-14). The tabernacle itself was a tent constructed of ten curtains of fine-twined linen and of blue, purple, and scarlet materials with cherubim skillfully woven into the fabrics. Each curtain was twenty-eight cubits long and four cubits wide (26:1,2). Careful instructions were given for fastening the curtains together (26:3-6). These curtains served as a kind of inner lining, for curtains of goats' hair (a standard Bedouin material for making tents) were to be put over them (see 26:7-11 for number and size of the curtains and how they were to be joined together to form the entire tent). The goats' hair curtain was longer than the inner tapestry curtain by two cubits; therefore, when hung across the wooden frame, it would reach a cubit lower on either side of the tapestry to cover it (26:12,13). Then a third covering of rams' skins and badgers' skins (see comment at 25:5) was to be made, apparently to serve as additional protection against the elements (26:14).

b) *The wooden frame* (26:15-30). It was necessary to build a frame over which the curtains could be draped and fastened. The individual sections of the frame were of acacia wood overlaid with gold. The number of sections, dimensions, and specifications for joining them together were given to Moses (26:16-25). Bars of acacia wood overlaid with gold were made to fit through the rings in the panels of the framework that rested in silver pedestals ("sockets," KJV; "bases," RSV) on the ground that would hold the entire structure together securely (26:26-30). The entire tabernacle, a remarkable forerunner of prefabricated houses, could be quickly put together when the Israelites were not traveling and as easily disassembled when they were ready to move on to another place.

c) *The veil and the screen* (26:31-37). Instructions then were given for making a veil (from a word that means "to shut off," "to bar," or "a shrine") out of the same materials of blue, purple, and scarlet and fine-twined linen, interwoven with cherubim (cf. 26:1). The veil was hung in such a way as to divide the tabernacle into two sections — the Holy Place and the Most Holy — and was a symbol of God's unapproachability (26:33; cf. Matt. 27:51; Heb. 6:19,20; 9:7,8; 10:19-22 for the New Testament significance of the veil).

The ark of the testimony (see Exod. 25:10-22) was to be placed in the Most Holy Place behind the veil with the mercy seat resting on the ark (26:33,34). Outside the veil in the Holy Place the table for the Bread of the Presence was to be placed on the north side (see 25:23-30) and the lampstand on the south side opposite the table (25:31-40).

A screen was to be made of the same fine materials as the veil but without the cherubim. It would serve to cover the entrance to the tabernacle (26:36,37).

6. *The altar of burnt offering* (27:1-8)

With instructions for the tabernacle proper completed, the Lord then turned His attention to the area surrounding the tent. In the courtyard around the tabernacle the altar of burnt offering and the bronze laver were to be placed (though the latter is not mentioned until 30:17-21). The altar was to be made of acacia wood, five cubits long, five cubits wide, and three cubits tall and overlaid with bronze. It was much smaller than Solomon's altar (2 Chron. 4:1) or Ezekiel's (Ezek. 43:13-17). Horns (that is, horn-like projections) of one piece with the altar were to be made on each of the four corners of the altar to hold the sacrificial animal firmly in place. The origin of altar horns is unknown, although Canaanite and Assyrian altars with horns have been found. Perhaps they were a stylized symbol of the animals that were sacrificed on the altar. The horns were considered the most sacred part of the altar; the blood of the sin offering was applied to them (Lev. 4:7,18,25,30; Exod. 30:10); a fugitive seeking asylum could seize the horns and be spared (21:13,14; 1 Kings 1:50-53; but cf. 1 Kings 2:28-34 where Solomon did not observe the sanctity of the horns in the case of Joab). Utensils of bronze for the altar were also to be provided (27:3) together with a bronze grate (27:4,5). Poles of acacia wood overlaid with bronze were made that fitted through rings attached to the altar so that the altar could be transported from place to place (27:6,7).

7. *The court of the tabernacle* (27:9-19)

The courtyard, or outer enclosure, about the tabernacle was a rectangular open-air area one hundred cubits long from east to west and fifty cubits wide from north to south enclosed by curtains of fine-twined linen five cubits high which were fastened to pillars filleted with silver and set in bronze bases (27:9-15,18) that were secured by cords tied to pegs driven in the ground (27:19; cf. 35:18). The gate for the court, located on the east side, was a screen twenty cubits long of the same materials as the screen for the tent (27:16; cf. 26:36).

8. *Oil for the lamp* (27:20,21)

Oil for the lamp was to be of the purest beaten olive oil and was to be provided by the people (27:20). One of the priests' daily duties was to take care of the lamp. It is not certain whether the lamp was to be kept burning without interruption ("to burn always," 27:20), but since verse 21 says they were to tend it from "evening to morning," the lamp probably was trimmed and lit each night and provided with enough oil to keep it burning till morning (cf. 1 Sam. 3:3). The tabernacle is called the "tent of meeting" for the first time in 27:21 (RSV and other translations; "tabernacle of the congregation," KJV), the place where God would meet His people and communicate His will to them.

B. The Priestly Garments (28:1-43)

Priests were not unique to Israel. Ancient Sumeria, Assyria, Egypt, and Babylon all had very elaborate priesthoods. The origin of the priesthood in the ancient world cannot be traced, but it undoubtedly grew out of a felt need for superhuman help and the belief that not everyone could communicate directly with the deity. The earliest priests ministered exclusively to members of their own family, the priest usually being the father of the family. As the priesthood evolved, it usually became a hereditary office, as it did in Israel.

The major functions of the priests in Israel were to consult God to determine His will for the people or for an individual, to instruct the people in the law, to present the sacrifices to God, to exercise certain judicial responsibilities, and to serve as guardians of the sanctuary, its treasures, and sacred vessels.

When these men stood before the people as God's priests, they were a reminder to the people of God's presence among them and of His willingness to forgive and to guide them. It was only appropriate that the garments they wore should match the glory and beauty of the place in which they served. Therefore, with the specifications for the tabernacle completed, the Lord proceeded to describe to Moses the garments the priests would wear when they ministered before Him.

1. *Introduction and summary of garments to be made* (28:1-5)

The Lord ordered Moses to call together Aaron and his sons Nadab, Abihu (see Lev. 10:1,2 for the fate of the first two sons), Eleazar (succeeded his father as high priest, Num. 3:4; 20:25-29), and Ithamar in order to make the garments they would wear as priests. "Priest" is from a word *kohen*, whose meaning is uncertain; etymologies that have been proposed include "soothsayer"; "be firm"; "make prosperous"; "to bend down," hence, do homage; and "stand upright," hence, serve. Israelites filled with the "spirit of wisdom" (28:3) would be selected from among all the people to make the articles of priestly attire (28:4). Exodus 28 is devoted almost entirely to a description of the garments for Aaron, the high priest. Only a few verses (vv. 40-43) describe the garments of Aaron's sons, the ordinary priests.

2. The ephod (28:6-14)

The ephod was to be made of gold and of the same fabrics as the veil (28:5,6; cf. 26:31). Though an ephod was sometimes an idol (Judg. 8:27) and sometimes an object that was consulted to learn the will of God (1 Sam. 23:9-11), here it seems to have been only a garment supported by two shoulder straps with a skilfully woven band (Exod. 28:8, RSV; "curious girdle," KJV) made of the same materials and used to fasten the ephod closely about the waist. Two onyx stones engraved with the names of the sons of Israel, six on each stone in the order of their age, were set in gold (28:11; "ouches of gold," KJV, but this is an archaic English word for the frame in which precious stones were set) and then attached to the shoulder straps to serve as stones of memorial (28:12). These stones served as symbols that the priest bore his people with him in his thoughts when he ministered before the Lord. Two chains of pure gold were attached to the settings (28:14).

3. The breastpiece (28:15-30)

A breastpiece of judgment was made of the same materials as the ephod (28:15). The KJV calls it a "breastplate," but this translation brings to mind a metal plate of armor. It was actually a kind of pouch, a span in length and width (about nine inches square) on which four rows of stones were affixed, three to a row, each a different precious or semi-precious stone (28:17-20), and each engraved with the name of one of the twelve tribes of Israel (28:21). Golden chains were placed through golden rings on the breastpiece in order to attach it firmly to the shoulder pieces and the ephod so it would lie flat on the priest's chest (28:25-28). Whenever Aaron went into the holy place, he was to wear the breastpiece of judgment over his heart to symbolize his constant remembrance of the twelve tribes before God.

The primary function of the breastpiece was to serve as a container for the Urim and the Thummim, which were kept in the breastpiece so that they would be over Aaron's heart when he went in before the Lord. The etymology of these two words is disputed. Urim was formerly considered to be from a word that means "lights," but today scholars believe it is from a word meaning "curse." Thummim is from a word that means "perfection." It is impossible to know what the Urim and Thummim looked like, but there is little doubt that they were used as sacred lots to determine the divine will in some way (cf. 1 Sam. 28:6).

4. Robe of the ephod (28:31-35)

The robe of the ephod was a sleeveless garment made of blue material of one piece with an opening for slipping it on over the head. Pomegranates of blue, purple, and scarlet material were arranged alternately with small golden bells as a border around the bottom of the robe. The pomegranate, a fruit common to Palestine and about the size of an orange, was a symbol of fertility in Canaan because of its many seeds, but it probably served only a decorative function on the priestly garments. The bells made it impossible for the priest to enter the holy God's presence unannounced, lest he die, and also they made it possible for the people outside to trace the movement of the priest within as he moved from place to place in the tabernacle.

5. The plate, turban, coat, and sash (28:36-39)

A plate (from a word "to blossom," or possibly "to shine"), an ornament of pure gold, was to be made and engraved with the words "Holy to the LORD" (28:36, RSV) and then fastened to the front of the high priest's turban (28:37; "mitre," KJV; literally, "that which is wrapped around") by means of a band of blue lace, or cord, tied around the turban. The words of the plate served as a reminder that the priest in a special way and all Israel represented through him were set apart for God's service. Furthermore, the guilt for any errors made in offering the holy things to God was placed upon the high priest (28:38).

The high priest's coat was to be woven of fine linen, as were his turban and sash (28:39, "girdle," KJV). According to the Talmud the sash, embroidered with needle work, was wrapped around the coat and was forty-eight feet long.

6. *Garments for the priests* (28:40-43)

In addition to the garments made for Aaron the high priest, coats, sashes, and caps (28:40; "bonnets," KJV) were to be made for Aaron's sons, as well as linen breeches, to cover their nakedness. It is not stated whether their garments differed from those of the high priest, except for the caps they wore instead of a turban, but they probably were much less elaborate. Both Aaron and his sons and all their descendants after them who would serve as priests were required to wear these garments whenever they went into the tent of meeting or approached the altar to minister in the holy place so they would not bring guilt on themselves and die (28:43).

God empowered Moses to anoint (28:41; from a word "to smear," a reference to the oil that was smeared or poured on a priest or king to set him apart for his work; the word "Messiah" comes from this word), consecrate (28:41; "ordain," RSV; literally, "fill their hand," probably a reference to filling their hands with the sacrifices they would present to the Lord), and sanctify (28:41; from a word, "to set apart") Aaron and his sons in order that they might begin their priestly duties.

C. Consecration of the Priests (29:1-46)

Having given the instructions for making the tabernacle and the priestly garments, the Lord then revealed to Moses the plans for the consecration ceremony that would set apart Aaron and his sons as priests of Israel. In future generations the priests would be in charge of consecrating other priests, but at Sinai there were no priests so it was appropriate that Moses, though not a priest himself, be given the unique honor of installing the first priests of the covenant people in his role as mediator of the covenant.

1. *Offerings, robing, and anointing* (29:1-9)

Moses was instructed to bring certain offerings (one young bull, two rams without blemish, and unleavened bread, cakes, and wafers) together with Aaron and his sons to the door of the tent of meeting to consecrate them (29:1; "hallow them," KJV, but translated as "sanctify" in 28:41). There he was to wash the priests with water (baptism probably finds its origin in these ritual lustrations), put Aaron's priestly garments on him (29:5, 6), and pour the anointing oil on his head (see 30:22-33 for the ingredients of the anointing oil). Then he was to put the garments on the sons that had been prepared for them. No mention is made of anointing the sons as well as the high priest, though 30:30 suggests that they were anointed, also.

2. *The sin offering for the priests* (29:10-14)

The bull was to be brought to the front of the tent of meeting where Aaron and his sons would lay their hands on its head before Moses killed it. This gesture symbolized identification with the animal, and the animal's death served as a substitute for the death of the worshiper. Part of the blood was to be smeared on the horns of the altar and the rest poured out at its base. The fat and certain other parts of the animal were to be burned on the altar, but the rest of the animal was to be burned outside the camp as a sin offering (cf. Lev. 4:1–5:13), suggesting that the sin had been transferred from the offerer to the animal, thereby securing forgiveness of sins.

3. *The burnt offering* (29:15-18)

Then, for the burnt offering, Aaron and his sons were to lay their hands on the head of one of the rams before it was slain by Moses. Its blood was to be sprinkled upon the altar, but after cutting up the animal and carefully washing the pieces, the entire animal was to be burned on the altar as a sweet savor (29:18; "pleasing odor," rsv; literally, "an odor that gives rest") and offering to the Lord. The whole burnt offering symbolized the complete dedication of the offerer to God (cf. Lev. 1:3-17).

4. *The ram of ordination* (29:19-34)

After Aaron and his sons laid their hands on the second ram, Moses was to kill it and take part of its blood and put it on the tips of the right ears of Aaron and his sons, and upon the thumbs of their right hands and upon the large toes of their right feet and then sprinkle the rest of the blood upon the altar (29:20; cf. Lev. 8:23,24). It has been suggested that the ritual symbolically means that the ear consecrated by blood listens to God's words, the thumb does God's work, and the toe walks in God's ways. However, blood smeared on the extremities of the body may be intended only to symbolize the cleansing of the entire body of the priest. As a further part of the consecration, Moses was to take part of the blood that was on the altar and some of the anointing oil and sprinkle them on Aaron and his garments and on his sons and their garments (29:21) so that their garments also would be consecrated. Then Moses was to place the fat of the ram and certain other parts of the animal (29:22), one loaf of bread, one cake of bread with oil, and one wafer (cf. 29:2,3) in the hands of Aaron and his sons to be waved back and forth for a wave offering before the Lord. The offerings were waved toward the altar and back, rather than from side to side, to symbolize that the offering was first given to the Lord and then returned to the priest for his use. Ordinarily the wave offering became food for the priests, but on this occasion it was to be burned on the altar (29:25), with the exception of the breast and the thigh ("shoulder," KJV), which were to be the priests' portion forever (29:26-28; cf. Lev. 7:30-36).

Aaron's priestly garments would be passed from generation to generation to the son (ordinarily the eldest) who would serve in his place (29:29). The garments would be worn only during the seven days required for the consecration (29:30; cf. 29:35; also see Lev. 16:4, 23,24, which indicate they were used annually).

The flesh of the second ram then was to be boiled, and Aaron and his sons would eat it at the entrance of the tent of meeting together with the bread remaining in the basket. No one else could eat this flesh, and any flesh or bread that remained till morning had to be burned because they were holy (29:34; cf. this shared meal with the peace offering, Lev. 3:1-17).

5. Repetition of ceremony for seven days (29:35-37)

The consecration ritual was repeated for seven days (seven was the number of completeness). Every day a bull was to be offered as a sin offering for atonement (from a word "to cover"), and a sin offering was to be made for the altar to cleanse it ("un-sin" it). Whatever touched the altar would become holy (an injunction interpreted as meaning that it would have to be destroyed because it has been affected by the holiness of the altar; however, cf. Hag. 2:12, which suggests that holiness is not contagious under some circumstances).

6. Morning and evening sacrifices (29:38-46)

Beginning with verse 38 instructions for daily sacrifices are given that were not related to the ordination ceremony of Aaron and his sons, perhaps as a reminder to the people that the covenant was maintained only through sacrifices. These verses describe sacrifices that were to be presented at the entrance of the tent of meeting morning and evening throughout all generations (cf. Num. 28:3-8). The morning sacrifice was to be a lamb offered with fine flour, beaten oil, and wine (29:40). The evening sacrifice was to be a lamb offered together with a grain offering and drink offering, as in the morning (29:41). God promised Moses that He would meet him at the tent of meeting to speak with him, and He also would meet the Israelites there. He would dwell among the children of Israel and be their God, and they would know that He was the Lord their God who brought them out of Egypt (29:46; cf. the Book of Ezekiel, where the phrase, "they/you will know that I am the LORD," is found sixty-six times, usually in the context of a warning that as a result of God's coming judgment Israel will know that He is the Lord).

D. Other Instructions (30:1-38)

1. *The altar of incense* (30:1-10)

Instructions then were given for making the altar of incense, which we would have expected to be included earlier along with the instructions for the tabernacle and its furnishings. The altar was to be made of acacia wood, one cubit long and one cubit wide, two cubits high, and overlaid with pure gold, with horns on the corners and a molding of gold around it. A golden ring was to be affixed to the two opposite sides into which poles made of acacia wood and overlaid with gold could be fitted for carrying the altar from place to place. It was to be placed in front of the veil that separated the Holy Place from the Holy of Holies (30:6). However, Hebrews 9:4 says the altar of incense was inside the veil, near the ark.

As part of his priestly duties Aaron would burn fragrant incense on the altar every morning when he refilled the lamps and again in the evening when he lit the lamps. No unauthorized incense (30:9; "strange incense," KJV; the same word is found in Leviticus 10:1-3 which speaks of "strange fire" offered by Nadab and Abihu that brought about their deaths) was to be offered on it. Neither were burnt offerings, grain offerings, or drink offerings to be offered on it. Aaron was required to make an atonement upon its horns once a year with the blood of the sin offering (Lev. 16:1-34; 23:26-32). Symbolically, the ascending smoke of burning incense has been interpreted as representing prayers offered to God.

2. *A census tax* (30:11-16)

The Lord also spoke to Moses concerning the taking of a census. The Israelites were allowed to take a census of the people from time to time, but when they did, it was necessary to give an offering (30:12;

literally "give a ransom," from the same word as "atonement") of half a shekel for each person twenty years of age and older who was counted so that no plague from God would fall on the people. Rich and poor alike paid the same amount, perhaps as a reminder that the privileges of worship were equally available to all. The money received would be used for the service of the tabernacle (30:16). When David took a census of the people (2 Sam. 24), a terrible punishment was inflicted upon them by the Lord. Though no explanation is given as to why God punished the Israelites on that occasion, it is possible that David overlooked the payment of the census tax required by the law of 30:11-16.

3. *The bronze laver for washing* (30:17-21)

As a further symbol of the holiness of God and of everything that pertained to the sacrificial system, the Lord instructed Moses to make a laver of bronze and to place it in the courtyard between the tent of meeting and the altar. Its dimensions are not given (cf. 1 Kings 7:23-39 for the size and number of lavers in Solomon's temple). It was to be filled with water and used by the priests to wash their hands and feet before entering the tent of meeting or performing their priestly duties. The priest who overlooked this ritual cleansing would die, for he had violated the holiness of God. The laver clearly symbolized the necessity of cleansing in order to enter the presence of God.

4. *The anointing oil* (30:22-33)

The various rituals of the tabernacle made use of either blood, water, or oil as symbols of consecration. In these verses is found the "recipe" for making the sacred anointing oil that was to be used for the consecration of the priests. The ingredients were myrrh (resin from a certain kind of tree not native to Palestine), sweet-smelling cinnamon, sweet cane (30:23; "sweet calamus," KJV), cassia (the aromatic bark of a tree much like cinnamon), and olive oil. Estimates have been made of the amount of anointing oil that would be made from the ingredients that vary from thirty-seven to one hundred pounds. The anointing oil was to be placed on various articles connected with the tabernacle as well as on the priests themselves, as a symbol of their identification with God's holiness (see 30:26-28 for a list of things to be consecrated with the oil). This sacred oil was never to be poured on the flesh of anyone who was not a priest. Whoever made anointing oil according to this formula or put it on an unauthorized person would be "cut off from his people"

(30:33; see 12:15 for explanation of this expression).

5. *Incense for the altar* (30:34-38)

No detail of the tabernacle was to be left to the imagination of the people. Even the formula for the incense to be burned on the altar of incense was given. It was to be made of equal parts of sweet spices, stacte (some kind of fragrant oil from a plant whose identity is uncertain). Onycha (obtained from a marine animal still gathered along the coasts of the Red Sea). Galbanum (an aromatic resin obtained from a plant of the carrot family), and frankincense (a fragrant resin obtained from several species of shrubs and trees). It was blended and seasoned with salt (perhaps because of its purifying qualities, or to make it burn more rapidly, or as a symbol of faithfulness). Salt also was an ingredient in the grain offering (Lev. 2:13). As with the anointing oil, so the Israelites were warned not to make this particular incense for personal use (Exod. 30:37,38).

E. Appointment of the Craftsmen (31:1-11)

The tabernacle and everything connected with it, including the articles of gold, silver, and bronze, the priestly garments, the anointing oil, and the incense were all to be made by a man called by God to the task by the name of Bezalel (Bezaleel, KJV; a name that means "in the shadow of God," that is, in God's protection), of the tribe of Judah and a descendant of Caleb (1 Chron. 2:19,20). The Lord told Moses that He had filled Bezalel with the spirit of God (the Old Testament uses this phrase only two other times, Exod. 28:3; 35:31), with wisdom, understanding, knowledge, and craftsmanship to enable him to do the work. Along with him the Lord set apart a man named Oholiab (Aholiab, KJV, a name that means "the father is my tent"), of the tribe of Dan, and also others who would help in the work.

F. The Keeping of the Sabbath (31:12-17)

In Genesis 17:11 circumcision was given as a sign of the covenant between God and Abraham. Now at Sinai God instructed Moses to tell the people to keep the Sabbath, for it was a sign for all future generations that they might know the Lord had set them apart (Exod. 31:13). It would also be a perpetual sign between God and the people of the fact that in six days He created heaven and earth and on the seventh He rested (31:17). The significant addition to the Sabbath law here, not found in 20:8-11, is the warning that whoever profaned the Sabbath by working on that day would be put to death (cf. Num. 15:32-36; John 5:16-18).

G. Conclusion: The written tables of stone given to Moses (31:18)

When God finished speaking to Moses on Mount Sinai, having given him the laws and the instructions for the tabernacle and the priests, He gave him the two tables of the testimony (the Decalogue) made of stone that had been written "with the finger of God" (31:18; see 8:19 for discussion of this phrase). Whatever else it suggests, it clearly identifies God as the source of and authority for the law given to Moses.

Volumes have been written on the spiritual teachings that can be adduced from a study of the tabernacle. The rich religious insights to be gained from such a study can only be suggested here. Throughout these chapters we are reminded that the laws are God's words and that they embrace all areas of life and work. The pattern of the tabernacle implies perfection by its design, symmetry, and dimensions. The dominating theme of the tabernacle is how to approach God. The graduated progression from the profane (beginning at the entrance on the east) to the outer court (with its altar and bronze laver) to the Holy Place (with its table for the Bread of the Presence, altar of incense, and lampstand) to the Most Holy Place (with its ark and mercy seat) vividly illustrates how a holy God must be approached. The prescribed garments and responsibilities of the priests, the acts of worship that included sacrifices and offerings, the involvement of worshiper and priest, and the different materials and metals used in the construction of the tabernacle are all instructive also. The climactic and greatest lesson of the tabernacle is that the presence of God dwelt in the midst of His people, and that He loved them and provided forgiveness for them.

For Further Study

1. In a Bible dictionary or encyclopedia (see bibliography) read articles on the tabernacle, ark of the covenant, Bread of the Presence (shewbread), priest, Ephod, Urim and Thummim, anointing.

2. Study a plan of the tabernacle found in one of the Bible encyclopedias and try to determine the significance of each of the furnishings.

3. Study the major responsibilities of the priests as they related to God and to the people.

4. Make a study of the concept of the holiness of God as found in the Old Testament.

5. Make a study of Ezekiel's visionary temple (Ezek. 40-43) and compare it to the pattern of the tabernacle.

PART FOUR: REBELLION AND RENEWAL

Chapter 10

Israel's Apostasy and Moses' Intervention
(Exodus 32:1–34:35)

While Moses was on Mount Sinai receiving the law from God, the people below were not idle. The longer Moses delayed his return, the more restless they became. They finally convinced themselves that Moses was not going to return and they were determined to make gods to worship that they could see and touch. Chapters 32-34 give the account of Israel's apostasy and stand as a kind of parenthesis between the instructions for building the tabernacle and the account of its actual construction. The episode serves as another reminder of the faithlessness of the people which would continue to characterize them even after they settled down in the Promised Land.

A. The Golden Calf (32:1-35)

1. *The people's apostasy* (32:1-6)

When Moses failed to return, the people concluded that something had happened to him and went to Aaron as the next-in-command with a demand that he make other gods *(elohim)* they could serve (32:1). The word *elohim* could be translated here "gods" or "a god"; either word would be appropriate, though the plural form of the verb "shall go" favors "gods." The Israelites were finding it difficult to adjust to the leadership of an invisible God and seemed to be deliberately repudiating Him by attributing their deliverance from Egypt to Moses (32:1). More inexplicable than the people's faithlessness was Aaron's acquiescence. He instructed them to bring their golden earrings, probably part of their loot from Egypt, from which he fashioned a molten calf with a graving tool (32:4), a metal instrument used to shape the idol after the gold had been melted down into a molten lump (cf. Judg. 8:24-27, where Gideon made an ephod of the gold earrings the people brought him). A better translation of "calf" would be "young bull," the symbol of vigor, strength, and reproductive power in the ancient world. When he presented the image to them, they acclaimed, "These be thy gods, O Israel, which brought thee up out of the land of Egypt" (32:4; cf. Ps. 106:19,20). Almost identical words are found in 1 Kings 12:28 when Jeroboam made two golden calves for Dan and Bethel.

Aaron then built an altar in front of the idol and proclaimed the next day as a "feast to the LORD" (Exod. 32:5). Notice that Aaron used the covenant name, Yahweh, so the episode should be interpreted only as a violation of the second commandment (20:4) and not the first (20:3). Apparently Aaron did not believe that what he had done was an outright rejection of God. The celebration that followed the next day was nothing less than an uninhibited sexual orgy associated with ancient fertility rites, only hinted at in the phrase "rose up to play" (32:6; cf. Gen. 26:8, where the same word is used with sexual overtones).

2. Moses' intercession (32:7-14)

At this moment God broke off His conversation with Moses and ordered him to go down to "your people." This was a subtle but deliberate disclaimer that they were any longer His people, to which Moses responded that they were "your people" (32:11)! God told Moses of the unrestrained revelry that was taking place below among the "stiffnecked people" (32:9, literally, "hard of neck"), a figure used to describe an ox or horse that stubbornly refuses to respond to the rope when tugged. The Lord was ready to destroy all the Israelites and raise up a great nation from Moses and his descendants (32:10), thereby fulfilling the promises made to Abraham (Gen. 12:2) and Jacob (Gen. 35:11). The covenant people would have become known in subsequent history as the children of Moses rather than the children of Israel.

The offer surely would have tempted a lesser person, but Moses was unwilling to profit at the expense of his people, wayward as they were. The preservation of Israel was more important to him than any personal advancement. His was the true shepherd's heart (cf. Ezek. 34 for a description of the shepherd who cares nothing for the sheep and John 10:1-16 for the description of a true shepherd). He could not desert the sheep so he "besought the Lord" (Exod. 32:11; the phrase literally means "to soften or make sweet the face of the Lord"). Moses' appeal to God was threefold: 1) Israel was God's people whom He had delivered from Egypt (Exod. 32:11); 2) His honor must be preserved so that the

Egyptians would have no occasion to accuse Him of being evil (32:12); and 3) the promises He had made to Abraham, Isaac, and Jacob must be kept (32:13). Moses' intercession was effective, for the Lord "repented of the evil which he thought to do unto his people" (32:14). The Hebrew word for "repentance" *(nacham)* as used of God in the Old Testament (cf. Gen. 6:6) does not imply that God makes mistakes and later acknowledges His error; the word conveys only the idea of grief or sorrow that leads to a different course of action. The passage teaches two lessons: 1) the efficacy of prayer and 2) the compassion of God even when man deserves punishment.

3. *The wrath of Moses* (32:15-20)

Moses departed from the presence of God with the two tablets of the law in his hand, written on both sides (Exod. 32:15). Tablets usually were inscribed on one side only, so this was a way of saying that these tablets were unique. On the way down the mountain Moses was rejoined by Joshua (see 24:13), who informed him that there was a "noise of war" in the camp (32:17). However, it was not a shout of military victory or a cry of defeat they were hearing but the sound of singing and revelry. When Moses approached the camp and saw the golden calf and the people dancing, he was furious. He smashed the tablets on the ground, not just as a rash display of anger, but probably to show that the covenant had been annulled by Israel's disobedience. Then he picked up the golden calf, threw it into the fire to melt it down to a shapeless lump of gold, then ground it to powder, mixed it with water, and forced the Israelites to drink the mixture (cf. 2 Kings 23:15). This dramatic act has been variously interpreted: 1) as a curse pronounced on the people that resulted in a plague (Exod. 32:35), 2) as a variation of the ordeal of jealousy that was used to determine if a wife had been faithless to her husband (Num. 5:11-31), or 3) as a demonstration of the total helplessness of the god (burned, crushed, mixed with water, and swallowed!). The greatest irony of the whole scene was having to drink one's own god, a lesson surely not lost on the Israelites.

4. *Aaron's excuses* (32:21-24)

Then Moses turned on Aaron and accused him of being responsible for the people's sin. Aaron passed the blame to the people (shades of Gen. 3!) by accusing them of being determined to do evil. He even suggested that there was something miraculous about the way the idol came into being (32:24). One wonders whether Aaron's sin here was not much more serious than the sin recorded in Numbers 20 that kept him from entering the Promised Land. Because Aaron's response seems so unbelievable, one commentary suggested that he was mocking Moses. However, the excuses we make when we try to justify our sins are probably every bit as transparent and absurd in the eyes of God.

5. *Faithfulness of the Levites* (32:25-29)

When Moses saw that the people were completely out of control (32:25; "naked," KJV, but the word is descriptive of their total behavior), he appealed for those who were on the Lord's side (32:26; literally, "Who is for the Lord?") to rally around him. Only the Levites, Moses' own tribe, joined him, and with sword in hand they killed three thousand of the worst offenders that day (1 Cor. 10:8 says 23,000 were killed). The spirit of dedication manifested by the Levites in caring more for God than for their own kinsmen (cf. Matt. 12:46-50) showed they were qualified for the priestly role they would soon assume.

6. *Moses' renewed intercession* (32:30-35)

The next day Moses bitterly denounced the people for their sin but added that he would return to the Lord to try to make atonement (32:30; literally "cover"; same word found in 29:36) for their sin. In the encounter that followed, Moses pleaded with the Lord to forgive them (32:32; literally, "lift up," one of several words in the Old Testament that mean forgiveness). If not, he insisted on being blotted out (cf. Ps. 51:1 for the same word and Rom. 9:3 for the same selfless attitude expressed by the apostle Paul) from the book the Lord had written. "To blot out" here may mean simply "to die," or it may be one of several references in the Bible to a book in which God has inscribed names of those who belong to His kingdom (Mal. 3:16; Pss. 69:28; 139:16; Luke 10:20; cf. Phil. 4:3; Rev. 3:5; 13:8; 20:12 , where it has become the "book of life"). Many ancient cities kept registers of their citizens (Isa. 4:3; Jer. 22:30; Ezek. 13:9); if one was not enrolled in the official register, he did not enjoy the rights and legal protection afforded a citizen.

God's rejection of Moses' offer made it clear that no person can atone for the sins of another. "Whosoever hath sinned against me, him will I blot out of my book" (32:33). This doctrine of individual responsibility for one's sins would later be clearly enunciated by Jeremiah (31:29,30) and Ezekiel (18:1-32; 33:10-20). The Lord did, however, reaffirm His promise to take the people to the Promised Land under Moses' leadership and said His angel would go before them (Exod. 32:34). The ambiguous language has been interpreted to mean that God Himself would no longer personally accompany His people. However, since the angel of the Lord is so closely identified with God Himself (see discussion at 3:1-6), and since 14:19 and 23:23 speak of the angel of the Lord accompanying His people at a time when God was not angry with Israel, the words may just as well be understood as a promise of the renewal of God's presence with His people. God inflicted further punishment on the people by sending a plague upon them (32:35; literally, "he struck the people").

B. The Promise of God's Presence (33:1-23)

1. *His presence withdrawn* (33:1-6)

Once again God reaffirmed the promise He had made to the patriarchs to bring the Israelites into the Promised Land (33:1; cf. Gen. 12:1; 35:12), a land flowing with milk and honey (Exod. 33:3; cf. 3:8; 13:5). This time, however, He added that He would not go up among them, lest by His proximity He would be unable to restrain His anger and destroy them. The sin of the golden calf had cost Israel the privilege of traveling with God in their midst. The people mourned when they heard the "evil tidings" (33:4; literally "this evil word") and removed their ornaments at God's direction to await His further decisions concerning them. The removal of the ornaments could be interpreted as a usual custom in time of grief, but it is quite possible that the ornaments were amulets associated with other deities (cf. Gen. 35:4).

2. *The tent of meeting* (33:7-11)

God had not really abandoned His people but now would only travel outside the camp and would meet Moses at a tent pitched outside the camp (called the "tabernacle of the congregation," KJV, but "tent of meeting" in most other versions). Those who sought the Lord to worship Him or to seek help from Him had to go outside the camp to the tent (33:7), thus serving as a constant reminder that God was displeased with the faithless people and that sin had separated them from Him. Scholars differ as to the identity of this tent. Some believe that it is another, but earlier, way of referring to the tabernacle (cf. Num. 4:3, where it clearly has become another name for the tabernacle). Some think that it is a simpler forerunner of the more elaborate tent described in chapters

25-31 (cf. 27:21, where the tabernacle is called the "tent of meeting"). Others believe, however, that it was Moses' private tent, pitched outside the camp, where God would meet him and speak with him face to face as a person would speak to a friend (33:11a). Joshua remained on guard at the tent whenever Moses went into the camp (33:11b).

3. *Moses' daring requests* (33:12-23)

Perhaps the boldest intercessory prayer in the Bible is found in these verses, which contain Moses' response to the Lord's announcement that He would not go up in the midst of the people. Moses seemed uncertain about the identity of the one who would be sent to lead them (33:12). He boldly reminded God of their past relationship — God had known him by name and had shown him favor. As proof of this relationship, Moses asked to know the ways of the Lord so that he might know better how to please Him.

The Lord's response (33:14) seems to imply: "Do you want to know Me better? Isn't it sufficient that My presence (literally, "My face") is with you?" Then He added as further assurance, "I will give thee rest" (33:14b), probably to be understood as a promise of the successful completion of the journey and possession of Canaan. Moses responded by emphasizing the necessity of God's presence with His people. Moses was ready to abandon the journey unless that presence went with him (33:15). The continued presence of God was the only way Moses could know that he had found favor in God's sight, and the only thing that would show that Israel was distinctive (33:16, "separated," KJV, a word that means "to be treated differently") from all other peoples in the world. For Moses the only thing that mattered was the presence of God; no accomplishment or success had meaning apart from that fact. What was true for Moses ought to be affirmed by every Christian — the only way people will know that a Christian is different is by that indefinable quality that is nothing less than the presence of God in him.

The Lord responded to Moses' daring words by agreeing to his request for a full restoration of the people, whereupon Moses made an even bolder request, "I beseech thee, shew me thy glory" (33:18; see discussion on 20:12 for meaning of the word "glory"). Perhaps Moses felt a need for reassurance that God's presence was still with him, or a need for a fresh vision of God, if he was to continue as the leader of Israel. Moses was asking no less than a full manifestation of God in all His majesty!

In a reply that can be interpreted only as evidence that God's anger had abated and that Israel's sin had been forgiven, He said, "I will make all my goodness pass before thee" (33:19; cf. v. 22, where His goodness is equated with His glory). Since God is totally good, He was agreeing to a full revelation of His being. He added, "I will proclaim the name of the LORD before thee" (33:19). The name was a revelation of the nature or character of a person (see 3:13-22 for additional discussion), and so God was promising to Moses an unprecedented revelation of Himself. Then as a reminder of His sovereignty, He added, "I will be gracious to whom I will be gracious, and will shew mercy on whom I will shew mercy" (cf. Hos. 11:9; Rom. 9:15). The sovereignty of God permits Him to bestow His favor on whomever He will, even on the worst sinner (Eph. 2:8,9; 1 Tim. 1:15).

Then as a warning that there are limitations on revelation, not because God is limited but because of the creaturely limitations of man, the Lord said, "You cannot see my face; for man shall not see me and live" (Exod. 33:20, RSV), an idea frequently expressed in the Old Testament (Gen. 16:13; 32:30; Deut. 4:33; Judg. 6:22,23; 13:22; Isa. 6:5). No one can know all about God, not even a Moses. There is a hiddenness about Him, even greater than between two people who say, "We see each other," and yet never really see more than a hint of the other.

To prepare Moses for the revelation, God told him He would direct him to a cleft in the rock on Mount Sinai where He would cover Moses with His hand until He passed by. Then after He passed, He would remove His hand, and Moses would be permitted to see His back but not His face (Exod. 33:22,23). In these verses God is spoken of in human terms (an anthropomorphism), but how else could human vocabulary begin to describe Him? Whatever else the almost unfathomable words mean, they suggest that the mystery of God can only be dimly and partially grasped in human experience. The enigma of God's hiddenness is unlocked in the New Testament when Jesus said, "Anyone who has seen me has seen the Father" (John 14:9, NIV).

C. Renewal of the Covenant (34:1-35)

When God first appeared to the Israelites at Sinai and offered to make a covenant with them, it was conditioned upon acceptance of His terms expressed in the laws given them. The people affirmed the covenant with the words, "All the words which the LORD hath said will we do" (24:3). But they had broken the covenant in the matter of the golden calf, so if they were to be reinstated as the covenant people, the covenant had to be renewed. Chapter 34 gives the account of the renewing of that relationship.

1. *The appearance of God before Moses* (34:1-9)

The Lord instructed Moses to hew two tables of stone to replace the ones Moses had smashed (32:19), on which He would again write the words of the law (34:1). He told Moses to ascend Mount Sinai the next day alone; even the flocks and herds were not to graze near the mountain (34:3). Moses did as he was instructed, and there on the mountain God again appeared to him in the cloud. He passed before him, as He had promised, and proclaimed His name: "The LORD, the LORD God, merciful and gracious, longsuffering, and abundant in goodness and truth" (34:6). The "name of the Lord" summarizes all that He is and does. Verses 6 and 7 contain a summary of the chief attributes of God. They emphasize both His righteousness that requires punishment of wrongdoing and His love that permits forgiveness (cf. 20:5,6; Jonah 4:2). Martin Luther called these verses "The sermon on the name of the Lord."

When Moses saw the unprecedented manifestation of God, he bowed low and worshiped. He then renewed his appeal to the Lord to go with the people, even though they were stiffnecked (cf. Exod. 32:9), to forgive them, and to take them for His inheritance (34:9).

2. *Conditions and laws of the covenant* (34:10-28)

The Lord's response was to agree to enter into a covenant relationship with them once again (34:10). He promised to do great things through them, such as had never been seen, and to do "a terrible thing," that is, something of which people would stand in awe (34:10). Again He promised to drive out the inhabitants of Canaan (34:11) and warned Israel not to make a covenant with any of the inhabitants of the land, lest they be a snare that would lead Israel to ruin (34:12). All their altars and symbols of their religion must be destroyed, including their Asherim (34:13, RSV; "groves," KJV). The Asherim were the sacred trees or wooden posts that figured in the Canaanite cultic practices, perhaps images of Asherah, the Canaanite goddess of fertility. The Lord knew that it was necessary to drive the Canaanites out of the land, lest the Israelites be attracted to the sensuous practices of Baal worship and begin worshiping the Canaanite deities and allow their children to intermarry, thereby opening the way for future generations of Israelites to be enticed to worship other gods (34:15,16).

Verses 18-26 repeat in substance the words of 13:12,13 and 23:12-19 (cf. 34:18 with 23:15; 34:19 with 13:12; 34:20 with 13:13 and 23:15b; 34:21 with 23:12; 34:22 with 23:16; 34:23,24 with 23:17; 34:25 with 23:18; and 34:26 with 23:19) and may be understood as a brief summary of God's demands upon His people. They serve as a reminder that the basis of the covenant was obedience to God's laws. Attempts have been made to find a new Decalogue in these verses, but the efforts seem forced and unconvincing. Moses remained on the mountain for forty days and forty nights without food or water, writing the Ten Commandments on the stone tablets (34:28; cf. Deut. 10:10).

3. *The shining of Moses' face* (34:29-35)

When Moses returned from Sinai carrying the two tables of testimony, the skin of his face shone from the reflection of the divine glory (cf. the transfiguration of Jesus in Matt. 17:1,2). The word "shone" is found only in 34:29,30,35 in the Old Testament and is related to the word *qeren* that means "horn"; it could be translated "sent out horns" ("rays"). Jerome's literal translation of the word in the Vulgate ("He knew not that his face was horned") gave rise to the frequent representations by artists of Moses with horns protruding out of his head, the best-known example being Michelangelo's magnificent statue of Moses in Rome. However, Moses was completely unaware that his skin was glistening, an attitude consistent with the humility of this great man of God (cf. Num. 12:3). He serves as a reminder that the greatest men of God usually are those least aware of their own spirituality (cf. John the Baptist, John 1:21,27; Paul, 1 Tim. 1:15).

When Aaron and the people saw Moses, they were afraid to come near him until he called to them. When they had gathered around him, he told them everything the Lord had said to him on Sinai. When he finished speaking, he put a veil over his face so the people would not be uncomfortable in his presence. Thereafter, whenever he went into the presence of the Lord, he removed the veil, replacing it when he returned to the people. The veil has been compared to a mask worn by priests in many primitive religions to show they were representing the deity when they wore the mask, but the comparison does not seem valid here.

Though we are not told, the radiance of Moses' face surely must have served as a constant reminder to the people that he had actually talked with God and that he was God's authoritative representative and appointed leader for Israel.

In 2 Corinthians 3:7-18 Paul gives an allegorical interpretation to Moses' veil. He says that Moses wore it so Israel would not see the glow gradually fading away. He compared it to the dispensation of law that passed away, to be replaced by the greater splendor of the dispensation of the spirit. He further compared the veil to the blindness of Israel that remained to that day when they read their Scriptures, a veil that is removed only through Christ.

Four important lessons that can be learned from chapters 32-34 are: 1) sin separates from God; 2) no one is ever so far removed from the attraction of other gods that he can relax his guard; 3) success achieved that forfeits the presence of God is meaningless; and 4) other people will know when we are in close fellowship with God.

For Further Study

1. In a Bible dictionary or encyclopedia (see bibliography) read articles on Baal worship, Levites, Asherah, tent of meeting, glory of the Lord.

2. Make a study of intercessory prayer, answering such questions as "Why? How? When?"

3. With the help of books on Old Testament theology, make a list of the most important attributes of God as found in the Old Testament.

4. Make a careful study of the doctrine of repentance in the Old Testament as it is used of God and of man.

Chapter 11

Construction of the Tabernacle

(Exodus 35:1–40:38)

Chapters 35-40 tell how the instructions for the tabernacle given to Moses in chapters 25-31 were carried out. In many cases the two sections are verbatim, except for the substitution of the past tense for the future tense. Occasionally the wording of a phrase is different only by abridgment or a minor omission; some verses are omitted altogether, and sometimes the order is different.[1] The book closes with a lengthy section (39:32–40:38) not found in chapters 25-31. The discussion that follows will call attention only to the important differences in the two accounts.

A. Preparations for Carrying Out the Work (35:1–36:7)

1. *The Sabbath* (35:1-3)

The command to observe the Sabbath is a repetition of the instructions found in 31:12-17, though 31:12-14, 16,17 have been omitted. Its placement at the beginning of these chapters was deliberate and emphasizes the importance of the Sabbath. The prohibition against kindling fire on the Sabbath (35:3) is an addition and is not found elsewhere in the Old Testament (though it is implied in 16:23).

2. *The offerings* (35:4-29)

Moses invited the people to make voluntary offerings of materials needed for the tabernacle (cf. 25:1-9; the list of materials in 35:6-9 is identical with 25:2-7; 25:8,9 are not repeated). The invitation to the skilled workers in 35:10-19 is not found in chapters 25-31 and includes

---

[1] For a carefully detailed study of the differences in the two accounts see S. R. Driver, *The Book of Exodus* in *Cambridge Bible for Schools and Colleges* (Cambridge: University Press, 1953), pp. 376-378.

"every able man," not just Bezalel and Oholiab (35:10). The response of the people is recorded in 35:20-29, with no parallel, of course, in the earlier section. "Every one whom his spirit made willing" (35:21) brought the materials as freewill offerings to the Lord which Moses had requested (35:29), and women with ability were invited to spin the fabrics (35:25,26).

3. The craftsmen (35:30–36:7)

Moses announced to the people the appointment of Bezalel and Oholiab and others who would help them in the work (cf. 31:1-11; the enumeration of things to be made found in 31:7-11 is not repeated). The people responded so generously that Moses had to ask them to stop bringing their offerings (36:2-7; cf. 2 Cor. 9:7).

B. Building the Tabernacle (36:8-38)

The verses in the following section have been rearranged from chapters 25-31 to follow the logical order of construction. First, the tent itself was made, before any of the equipment (cf. 26:1-37). The incense altar is mentioned along with other articles placed inside the tent (cf. 30:1-10); and the bronze laver is included with the altar and courtyard, where it properly belongs (cf. 30:17-21).

1. The curtains for the tabernacle (36:8-13)

The curtains that formed the basic dwelling were made according to instructions given in 26:1-6.

2. The tent for covering the tabernacle (36:14-19)

The two protective coverings for the tent were then made according to the instructions given in 26:7-14 (26:9b,12,13 are not repeated).

3. The frame for the tabernacle (36:20-34)

The frames were made according to the instructions given in 26:15-29 (26:30 is not repeated).

4. The veil and the screen (36:35-38)

The veil and the screen were made according to the instructions given in 26:31-37 (26:33-35 is not repeated).

C. The Furnishings for the Tabernacle (37:1–38:20)

1. *The ark of the covenant* (37:1-9)

The ark and mercy seat were made according to the instructions given in 25:10-22 (25:15,16,21,22 are not repeated).

2. *Table for the Bread of the Presence* (37:10-16)

The table for the Bread of the Presence was made according to the instructions given in 25:23-29 (25:30 is not repeated). The bread to be placed on the table is not mentioned here, though it is included in the list in 39:23.

3. *The lampstand* (37:17-24)

The lampstand was made according to the instructions given in 25:31-40 (25:37b,40 are not repeated). The instructions for the oil for the lamp are not repeated (cf. 27:20,21).

4. *The altar of incense* (37:25-28)

The altar of incense was made according to the instructions given in 30:1-5 (30:6-10 with its reference to the Day of Atonement is not repeated).

5. *The incense and anointing oil* (37:29)

The incense and anointing oil were made according to the instructions given in 30:22-38. However, the instructions are condensed to a bare enumeration in one verse and 30:26-33,36-38 are not repeated.

6. *The altar of burnt offering* (38:1-7)

The altar of burnt offering was made according to the instructions given in 27:1-8a (27:8b is not repeated).

7. *The bronze laver for washing* (38:8)

The bronze laver was made according to the instructions given in 30:18-21 (30:18b-21 are not repeated and 38:8b, describing the women who ministered at the door of the tent of meeting is an addition (cf. 1 Sam. 2:22). The function of the mirrors and the nature of the women's service are unknown. Some have supposed that the mirrors were gifts of the women and that the women were responsible for cleaning and repairs or were singers and dancers.

8. *The court of the tabernacle* (38:9-20)

The court of the tabernacle was made according to the instructions given in 27:9-19 (there is some variation in the wording of the two accounts).

D. Summary of the offerings (38:21-31)

These verses contain an inventory of the metals used in the construction of the tabernacle and its furnishings and have no parallel in chapters 25-31. The amount of gold was twenty-nine talents and 730 shekels (38:24), about 1900 pounds. The amount of silver was 100 talents and 1775 shekels (38:25), about 6437 pounds. The silver collected represented half a shekel (a beka) for each person numbered in the census (cf. Num. 1:46). In Exodus 30:11-16 we are told that the half-shekel census tax was to be used for the service of the tent of meeting. The amount of bronze was seventy talents and 2400 shekels (38:29), about 4522 pounds. Altogether, the gold, silver, and bronze weighed more than six tons.

E. The Priestly Garments (39:1-31)

1. *Introduction* (39:1)

The first verse serves as an introduction to the account of the making of the priestly garments and has no parallel in chapters 25-31.

2. *The ephod* (39:2-7)

The ephod was made according to the instructions given in 28:6-14 (most of 39:3 is not found in the parallel account in 28:6-8; 28:9-12 is given in abridged form, and 28:13,14 is omitted altogether).

3. *The breastpiece* (39:8-21)

The breastpiece (shortened from "breastpiece of judgment"; cf. 28:15) was made according to the instructions in 28:15-30 (39:16a is an abridgment of 28:13,14, and 28:29,30, describing the Urim and Thummim, is not repeated).

4. *Robe of the ephod* (39:22-26)

The robe of the ephod was made according to the instructions in 28:31-35a (28:35b is not repeated).

5. *Other priestly garments* (39:27-31)

The other priestly garments were made according to the instructions in 28:36-43 (28:38,41,42b,43 are not repeated, however; and

28:39,40,42a are abridged). The plate inscribed with "Holy to the Lord" (28:36,37; 29:6) is here described as a crown (39:30).

F. Completion of the Tabernacle (39:32–40:38)

1. *Presentation of the work to Moses* (39:32-43)

When all the work was completed, everything was brought to Moses (see 39:33-41 for a complete list of the articles brought), and after examining everything to see that it had been made as the Lord had commanded, Moses blessed the people (there may be an intentional echo of Gen. 1:31 here of God pronouncing a benediction on His completed creation).

2. *Erection of the tabernacle* (40:1-33)

The Lord instructed Moses to erect the tabernacle of the tent of meeting on the first day of the month and to arrange all the furnishings in their proper places (40:1-8). Moses probably supervised the work, as it would have been difficult for one person to erect the tabernacle unaided. Then Moses was to anoint the tabernacle and everything that was in it with the sacred anointing oil (40:9-11; instructions for making the anointing oil given in 30:22-33 are omitted here). Then he was to bring Aaron and his sons to the door of the tent of meeting, wash them, put the holy garments on them, and anoint them so they could begin their priestly duties (40:12-15a; cf. Lev. 8; 9 for a detailed account of the consecration ceremony). The description of the consecration of the priests does not repeat the sacrifices described in chapter 29. The priesthood was to remain in Aaron's family for all time as a hereditary possession (40:15b; cf. 29:9).

Moses then carried out the Lord's instructions on the day that had been designated. According to 40:17 it was exactly a year since the Israelites had left Egypt (cf. 12:2,3) and nine months after their arrival at Sinai (19:1).

3. *God's presence in the tabernacle* (40:34-38)

When Moses finished the work and the priests were installed, the cloud covered the tent of meeting and the glory of the Lord filled the tabernacle (40:34; cf. Isa. 6:4; 1 Kings 8:11, where God's presence filled the temple, and Exod. 24:17,18 that describes the presence of God on Mount Sinai). The unusual manifestation was evidence that the Lord's presence was among His people and that He approved the work that had been done. Moses himself was not able to enter the tent because of the cloud and the glory (40:35). From that time on whenever the cloud was lifted up from over the tabernacle, the people would move on, but if the cloud was not taken up, they did not travel. Throughout the rest of their journey until they reached the Promised Land, the cloud of the Lord was on the tabernacle by day and fire was on it by night, visible to all the people (40:38; cf. Num. 9:15-23).

The Book of Exodus closes with the fulfillment of the promise of God's presence given in 29:45 and renewed in chapter 33. His presence would sanctify the Israelites, protect them, and bring them to their destination.

For Further Study

1. Why do you think chapters 25-31 are repeated almost verbatim in chapters 35-40?

2. Make a list of the most important differences in the two accounts of the construction of the tabernacle.

3. In what ways does God make His presence known today?

4. How can you account for the continued faithlessness of Israel in spite of the mighty deeds God did in her behalf?

5. See if you can summarize the Book of Exodus in a few minutes from memory.

6. Write out in summary sentences the major teachings of the Book of Exodus.

Bibliography

Commentaries on Exodus

Beegle, Dewey M. *Moses, the Servant of Yahweh* (Grand Rapids: William B. Eerdmans Publishing Co., 1972).

Childs, Brevard S. *The Book of Exodus* in *The Old Testament Library* (Philadelphia: The Westminster Press, 1974).

Clements, Ronald E. *Exodus* in *The Cambridge Bible Commentary on the New English Bible* (Cambridge: University Press, 1972).

Cole, R. Alan. *Exodus: An Introduction and Commentary* in *The Tyndale Old Testament Commentaries* (Downers Grove, Ill.: InterVarsity Press, 1973).

Driver, S. R. *The Book of Exodus* in *Cambridge Bible for Schools and Colleges* (Cambridge: University Press, 1953 reprint).

Honeycutt, Roy L., Jr. "Exodus," *The Broadman Bible Commentary*, vol. 1 (Nashville: Broadman Press, 1969).

Hyatt, J. P. *Exodus* in *New Century Bible* (London: Oliphants, 1971).

Keil, C. F., and Delitzsch, F. *The Pentateuch* in *Biblical Commentary on the Old Testament*, vol. 1 (Grand Rapids: William B. Eerdmans Publishing Co., 1959 reprint).

McNeile, A. H. *The Book of Exodus* in *Westminster Commentaries* (London: Methuen & Co., 1908).

Meyer, F. B. *Exodus: A Devotional Commentary.* 2 vols. (Grand Rapids: Zondervan Publishing House, 1952 reprint).

Ramm, Bernard L. *His Way Out: A Fresh Look at Exodus* (Glendale, Calif.: G/L Publications, 1974).

Rylaarsdam, J. Coert. "The Book of Exodus," *Interpreter's Bible*, vol. 1 (New York/Nashville: Abingdon Press, 1952).

Bible Dictionaries and Encyclopedias

Buttrick, George Arthur, ed. *The Interpreter's Dictionary of the Bible.* 4 vols. (New York/Nashville: Abingdon Press, 1962).

Douglas, J. D., ed. *The New Bible Dictionary* (Grand Rapids: Willam B. Eerdmans Publishing Co., 1970).

Orr, James, ed. *The International Standard Bible Encyclopedia.* 5 vols. (William B. Eerdmans Publishing Co., 1957 reprint).

Tenney, Merrill C., ed. *The Zondervan Pictorial Bible Dictionary,* rev. ed. (Grand Rapids: Zondervan Publishing House, 1967).

Tenney, Merrill C., ed. *The Zondervan Pictorial Encyclopedia of the Bible.* 5 vols. (Grand Rapids: Zondervan Publishing House, 1975).

Unger, Merrill F. *Unger's Bible Dictionary* (Chicago: Moody Press, 1957).

Bible Translations

King James Version. Referred to in the Study Guide as KJV.

New American Standard Bible (Carol Stream, Ill.: Creation House, Inc., 1971). Referred to in the Study Guide as NASB.

New Catholic Edition of the Holy Bible Translated from the Latin Vulgate (New York: Catholic Book Publishing Co., 1949-50). Referred to in the Study Guide as the Vulgate.

New International Version (Grand Rapids: Zondervan Bible Publishers, 1973). Referred to in the Study Guide as NIV.

Revised Standard Version (New York: Thomas Nelson & Sons, 1953). Referred to in the Study Guide as RSV.